D0618963

ROMÉ

StyleCity

ROME

With over 300 colour photographs and 6 maps

Thames & Hudson

detti uccellini matti, o scappati:

OLENTA PASTICCIATA ALLA VENETA

POLLO SPEZZATO COI PEPERONI

li macellari porteno l'anello,
li carettieri er fazzoletto ar collo
e lo mi' amore le penne ar capp

NOTIFICAZIONE

Contents

Street Wise

Style Traveller

Series concept and editor: Lucas Dietrich
Jacket and book design: Grade Design Consultants
Original design and map concept: The Senate
Maps: Peter Bull

Research and texts: Sara Manuelli
Specially commissioned photography by
Angela Moore

Although every effort has been made to ensure that
the information in this book is as up-to-date and as
accurate as possible at the time of going to press,
some details are liable to change.

First published in the United Kingdom in 2005 by
Thames & Hudson Ltd, 181A High Holborn,
London WC1V 7QX

www.thamesandhudson.com

British Library Cataloguing-in-Publication Data
A catalogue record for this book is available from the
British Library

ISBN-13:   978-0-500-21015-4
ISBN-10:   0-500-21015-2

Printed in China

How to Use This Guide

The book features two principal sections: **Street Wise** and **Style Traveller**.

Street Wise, which is arranged by neighbourhood, features areas that can be covered in a day (and night) on foot and includes a variety of locations – cafés, shops, restaurants, museums, performance spaces, bars – that capture local flavour or are lesser-known destinations.

The establishments in the **Style Traveller** section represent the city's best and most characteristic locations – 'worth a detour' – and feature hotels (**sleep**), restaurants (**eat**), cafés and bars (**drink**), boutiques and shops (**shop**) and getaways (**retreat**).

Each location is shown as a circled number on the relevant neighbourhood map, which is intended to provide a rough idea of location and proximity to major sights and landmarks rather than precise position. Locations in each neighbourhood are presented sequentially by map number. Each entry in the **Style Traveller** has two numbers: the top one refers to the page number of the neighbourhood map on which it appears; the second number is its location.

For example, the visitor might begin by selecting a hotel from the **Style Traveller** section. Upon arrival, **Street Wise** might lead him to the best joint for coffee before guiding him to a house-museum nearby. After lunch he might go to find a special jewelry store listed in the **shop** section. For a memorable dining experience, he might consult his neighbourhood section to find the nearest restaurant crossreferenced to **eat** in **Style Traveller**.

Street addresses are given in each entry, and complete information – including email and web addresses – is listed in the alphabetical **contact** section. Travel and contact details for the destinations in **retreat** are given at the end of **contact**.

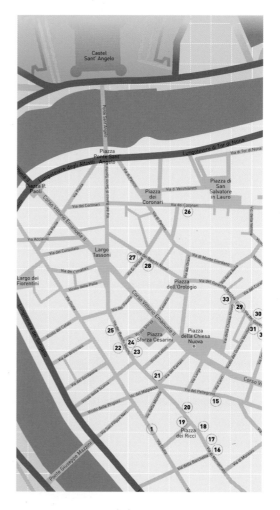

Legend

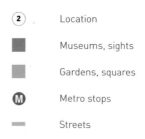

(2)   Location

    Museums, sights

    Gardens, squares

(M)   Metro stops

    Streets

ROME

Mesmerizing Rome, hub of an ancient empire. Medieval and Baroque, piled on a vision of crumbling antiquity and decadence. Aged political city, seat of papal power, hip epicentre of swinging post-war Europe. History marks Rome at every turn, it oozes on to the rambling succession of cobbled alleyways, squares and palaces that weave through its largely unspoiled historic centre.

The capital of modern Italy and host to the Vatican – the city within a city – Rome's population is around four million, but it feels distinctly un-modern and barely a metropolis. The wealth of centuries-old art and architecture seems to ward off even the tiniest modern advance. Rome still lives a village life: food and vegetable markets appear in every neighbourhood; craft shops, bars and piazzas act as community meeting points; cars creep around tiny streets best suited for walking. Rome has none of the boulevard ostentation of its European counterparts; instead, the atmosphere of a thriving, social, medieval city remains intact.

Founded on seven hills and now spread into a well-contained suburban sprawl, Rome is largely defined by its ancient centre, itself divided into quarters. Its many churches and palaces were restored to authentic Pompeiian reds, pale blues and ochres during the massive Millennium facelift that spruced up the city. Modish areas like Trastevere and Campo de' Fiori are the crowd-pullers, but they are gradually being usurped by Testaccio, the slaughterhouse area, now revitalized by a bustling nightlife scene, and San Lorenzo, home to the city's students and thriving artist community. A steady rise in property prices has pushed young, low-income bohemians into neighbourhoods like il Pigneto and Ostiense, set to become the creative and nightlife hotspots in the coming years.

A political city since the days of the Roman Empire, Rome bears its *Caput Mundi* (Head of the World) status lightly. Its citizens display a healthy disrespect towards the ruling class and use jaded sarcasm against excessive displays of wealth. Unlike its 'rival' Milan, Rome's inhabitants traditionally resist the northern European work ethic, something that has always given the city a reputation for being relaxed, if not cheerfully chaotic. An afternoon siesta is not as common as it once was, but most workers still take a whole hour for a leisurely lunch (including shopkeepers). *La Dolce Vita* living style might have just been Federico Fellini's idealization of a particular era, but it undoubtedly captured the heady mix of hedonism, laziness and the ability to reinvent oneself daily (*l'arte di arrangiarsi*) that defines the Roman way.

Rome's rich pot of culture can sometimes be overwhelming, but luckily many of the sights are easily accessible on foot. Casual wanderings can reveal magnificent art in tucked away churches. With the Baroque beauties of Borromini and Bernini, Michelangelo's architectural and pictorial masterpieces, the vast ruins of the Forum and the glittering Byzantine-style mosaics, the Eternal City offers many moments of rapture. And there are a few modern gems that should not be overlooked: try Mussolini's grand design, EUR, a satellite city intended to host the World Expo in 1942 and a celebration of the regime through monumental form. Political connotations aside, the EUR is an astonishing showcase of the Italian Rationalist style by architects such as Adalberto Libera and Marcello Piacentini. The Civiltà del Lavoro building – dubbed the 'Square Colosseum' by Romans because of its spectacular six floors of arcades – is a landmark of rigorous serenity. Mosaics by Futurist artists such as Fortunato Depero and Enrico Prampolini are just some of the often ignored treasures of the area, now due for regeneration with Rome-born architect Massimiliano Fuksas's plans for a new Congress Centre. The Esquilino, a grid of apartment blocks built in 1870 just after the unification of Italy, is the location of the Termini railway station, planned in the 1920s and completed after the Second World War. Today the station's recently renovated Kappa area hosts parties and events, while new shops, hotels and wine bars are transforming the station's image.

The city has suddenly taken a more cosmopolitan approach to design, with a spate of new restaurants and bars opting for a sleeker aesthetic. Style-seeking travellers are spoilt for choice for hotels, whether they opt for the more grandiose establishments near Piazza di Spagna or ultra-modern alternatives such as hotels Radisson SAS or Aleph (p. 130 and p. 128). No other building better represents the cultured and enlightened administrations of the past ten years than Renzo Piano's Auditorium and Parco della Musica (p. 42), inaugurated in 2002, which has acted as catalyst for Rome's cultural and architectural renaissance. Richard Meier's multi-award-winning church of Dio Padre Misericordioso in the suburb Tor Tre Teste is sacred architecture as its most modern, and symbolizes the city's aptitude for commissioning contemporary buildings. Forthcoming projects include Zaha Hadid's MAXXI arts centre and Odile Decq's extension of contemporary art museum Macro (p. 41).

Is there a city more photogenic than Rome? The city has a slow-paced beauty that lends itself to a cinematic backdrop: a creeper-clad wall, a sunset-tinged dome across the river at St Peter's, lovers perched on a sky-blue Vespa. Even through the snap of a digital camera, Rome is a vision steeped in antiquity and frozen in time.

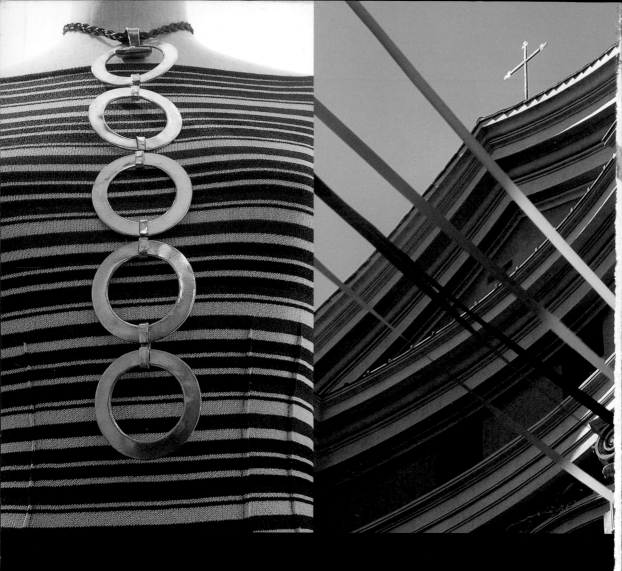

Street Wise

Pantheon
Piazza di Spagna
Via Vittorio Veneto

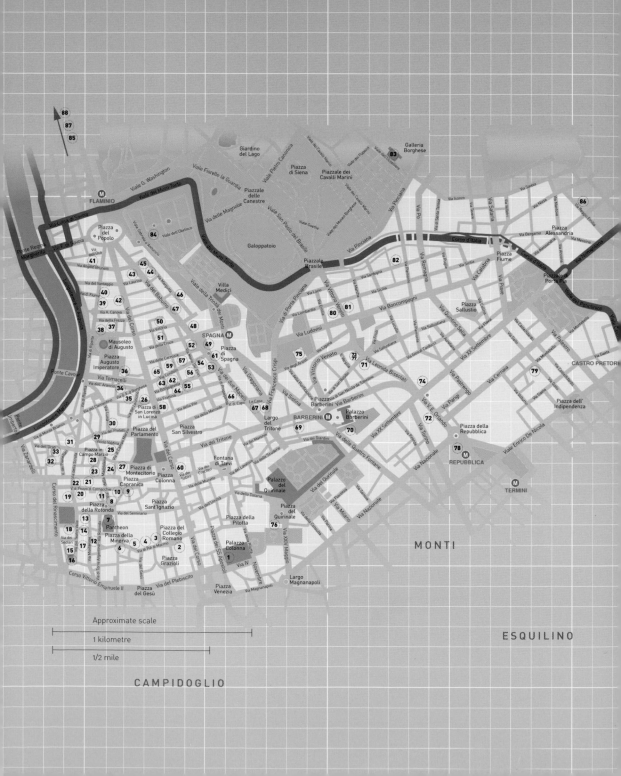

FLAMINIO Ⓜ

Giardino
del Lago

Piazza
di Siena

Piazzale dei
Cavalli Marini

Galleria
Borghese

83

86

Piazzale
delle
Canestre

Villa
Medici

Piazzale
Brasile

82

Piazza
Alessandria

Piazza
Fiume

Piazza di
Porta Pia

Piazza
Sallustio

Piazza
del Popolo

84

Galoppatoio

81

80

Piazza dell'
Indipendenza

CASTRO PRETORIO

41

45

44

43

46

47

Villa
della Trinità dei Monti

Via Ludovisi

75

77
71

74

79

40

39

42

50

51

48

SPAGNA Ⓜ

49

Piazza
di Spagna

72

38 37

Mausoleo
di Augusto

52

61

Piazza della
Repubblica

Piazza
Augusto
Imperatore

36

65

59

57

54

53

55

68

67

BARBERINI Ⓜ

78

34

63

62

56

64

66

Palazzo
Barberini

REPUBBLICA Ⓜ

35

26

58

69

70

Piazza di
San Lorenzo
in Lucina

Largo
del Tritone

30

Piazza del
Parlamento

Piazza
San Silvestro

Ⓜ **TERMINI**

31

29

33

25

24

27

Piazza di
Montecitorio

32

28

23

Piazza
Capranica

60

Piazza
Colonna

Fontana
di Trevi

Palazzo
del Quirinale

MONTI

22 21

19 20

11

10 9

Piazza
Sant'Ignazio

18

13 14

8

Piazza
della Rotonda

Piazza del
Collegio
Romano

Piazza della
Pilotta

Palazzo
del
Quirinale

76

7

12

17

Pantheon

4 3

Palazzo
Colonna

15

Piazza della
Minerva

5

2

16

6

Piazza
Grazioli

1

Piazza IV

Corso Vittorio Emanuele II

Piazza
del Gesù

Piazza
del Plebiscito

Piazza
Venezia

Largo
Magnanapoli

Approximate scale

1 kilometre

1/2 mile

CAMPIDOGLIO

ESQUILINO

88
87
85

Ancient, medieval and Renaissance Rome all come together here. The heady mix of history enclosed between the Pantheon and Via Vittorio Veneto is where most visitors flock to for glimpses of monuments and churches and to pick up a few items from the prime shopping centre of Rome. From Largo di Torre Argentina across to Via del Corso lies the Campo Marzio (Field of Mars), famous during Roman times for being the great monumental centre of the city, where baths and theatres, porticoes and arenas stood in a park-like setting of public gardens. Today, the Pantheon's perfectly engineered and voluminous dome is still a top attraction, while the smaller scaled but life-sized elephant by Bernini stands gracefully in Piazza della Minerva. Nearby, artisans' workshops, fashion boutiques such as Degli Effetti (p. 162) and historic cafés Sant' Eustachio (p. 153) and Tazza D'Oro (p. 152) create leisurely pedestrian trails for elegantly coiffured *signore* and starry-eyed tourists as well as the odd politician (Rome's parliament, Montecitorio, is a mere stone's throw away). But turn into a semi-hidden piazza to see life at a quieter pace: a feral cat dozing atop a parked Cinquecento and waiters slowly laying their outdoor tables at the bars and trattorias.

While the main stretch of Via del Corso is pretty much a succession of anonymous chain shops, the roads that slice across it are considered Rome's most luxurious shopping parade. Haughty fashion ateliers and tailors are hidden in the courtyards of Renaissance palazzi around Via Condotti and Via Frattina, while international brands like Gucci, Valentino (p. 175) and Bulgari (p. 170) have established their sleekly designed headquarters. Via del Babuino is a cut above the rest, with the 'concept store' TAD (p. 174) serving the discerning clientele of nearby hot locations Hotel de Le Russie and Hotel Art (p. 118). Past the pastel-tinted palaces to the Spanish Steps and climbing up above the throng of shoppers towards Villa Medici, today the seat of the French Academy, you can catch a glimpse of the city's mesmerizing rooftops and cupolas.

Beyond the luxury hotels that line Via Gregoriana is Via Vittorio Veneto, site of *La Dolce Vita*. The street may never regain the glamour of the 1950s but a revival is definitely under way. You only have to walk along Via di San Basilio to find the start of a contemporary design sensibility inspired by Adam Tihany's Aleph Hotel (p. 128), and eateries like San Marco (p. 39) and Moma (p. 34). The architectural future of the city, however, lies north, past the park of the Villa Borghese and its impressive museum. The recent art complex of Macro (p. 41), the soon to be completed Zaha Hadid MAXXI venue (p. 41) and Rome's jewel in the crown, the Renzo Piano designed Auditorium (p. 42), prove the eternal city's intention to catch up with other European metropolises.

BOOKS FOR KIDS

1 Mel Giannino Stoppani

Piazza dei Santissimi Apostoli 59–65

Mel Giannino Stoppani's bookstore is a children's paradise. Sleekly designed and filled with the best international literature for children of all ages, it has large English and French language sections. The toddler's room even features a small playing area where samples of books and toys distract offspring, allowing parents to purchase undisturbed. Illustrated books are the store's forte, especially classics by designers Bruno Munari and Enzo Mari, which are also popular with adult collectors. Italian author Gianni Rodari is another favourite, along with international bestseller J.K. Rowling. Games, posters, videos and DVDs are also available. On Saturdays, theatrical events, readings and parties entertain children over three years old.

FAMILY JEWELS

2 Galleria Doria Pamphilj

Piazza del Collegio Romano 2

No visit to Galleria Doria Pamphilj would be complete without Jonathan Pamphilj's audio guide. His commentary is not just a history of the collection, it's a delightful recollection of a childhood spent in a palazzo surrounded by paintings and sculptures steeped in history. Opened to the public since 1996, the Galleria houses an impressive collection of art, begun in the 17th century by the Pamphilj dynasty. There are masterpieces by Caravaggio, Guido Reni, Guercino and Velázquez and important Renaissance pieces by Titian and Raphael. The Pamphilj's married into other important aristocratic families and became one of the most influential families in Rome. Perhaps the most renowned family member was Pope Innocent X (1644–55), born Giovan Battista Pamphilj and immortalized in Velázquez's portrait, on show here, famously the inspiration for Francis Bacon's version.

CHOCOLATE BOX
3 **Confetteria Moriondo e Gariglio**
Via di Piè di Marmo 21 22

This historic chocolate shop was opened in 1886 by two Turinese chocolate masters who followed the Piedmontese Savoia kings to Rome. Decorated in a deep red with quaint wooden shelves, green ribbons and voile, it is the perfect container for truffles, *gianduiotti*, fruit jellies and marron glacés, all made on the premises. Easter is when the shop is at its busiest, and the assistants, wearing prim aprons and caps, scurry to and fro serving eager customers their multi-coloured hollow chocolate eggs. For St Valentine's Day, the store wraps its chocolates in the dainty heart-shaped boxes that were originally created to celebrate the engagement between Maria José and King Umberto Di Savoia.

SLOW-PACED FASHION
4 **Le Tartarughe**
Via di Piè di Marmo 17, 33
Via del Gesù 71a

Le Tartarughe is the sort of place where you might find the perfect trouser suit, a cleverly cut silk dress or a kaleidoscopic hand-knitted jumper. Its individualistic style is always elegant but never tied to the tyranny of fashion trends. Founded in 1972 by Susanna Liso, a theatre costume designer by training, Le Tartarughe was initially a capsule knitwear collection. Then in 1982 Susanna opened her womenswear shop in Via di Piè di Marmo and quickly gained a reputation among well-heeled Romans. In 2003 she opened the nearby accessories shop, with pieces by local craftsmen. Her third boutique, in Via del Gesù, specializes in one-off couture pieces.

For a privileged peek of the Roman rooftops that surround the domed Pantheon, head for the roof-bar of the Hotel Minerva, a luxury hotel housed in a 17th-century palazzo recently restored by architect Paolo Portoghesi. The hotel faces Piazza della Minerva's elephant obelisk and the church of Santa Maria sopra Minerva, which counts among its jewels Michelangelo's sculpture *Christ Bearing the Cross*. Take the lift up to the top floor where, amid the tenderly kept geraniums and roses on the spacious terrace, cocktails and light meals are served from noon to 2 a.m. every day. Early evening is a good time to visit if your taste does not run to background piano music. While sipping a Bellini, you would be forgiven for falling under the illusion that you owned one of the most panoramic views in town.

STUNNING DOME

7 Pantheon

Piazza della Rotonda

Despite Agrippa's inscription on the portico, the Pantheon was actually built in AD 118 during Hadrian's regime and may even have been designed by him. The building's dome, an admirable feat of Roman engineering, is more than forty-three metres high. It was the largest dome in the world until 1436 when the Duomo in Florence was constructed. In 609 the Pantheon was the first temple in Rome to be consecrated. It was renamed Santa Maria ad Martyres because of the many martyrs' bones that were buried beneath the new sanctuary, when, according to tradition, seven devils escaped the Christian site and one particularly large demon struggling to break free created the great oculus in the centre of the dome. It is the site of burial for the kings of Italy as well as the artist Raphael. The sheer size of the interior and its opulent marbles make the Pantheon look more like a monument than a church, except on Christmas Eve when a candlelit midnight mass and Gregorian chant create a rarefied atmosphere.

In a world dominated by mass production and digital communication, it is refreshing to know that the art of writing is still alive and kicking in the historic centre of Rome. Scribes and stationery addicts will delight in this 1930s family-run shop, recently returned to its original Art Déco style, with walnut fittings and floor-to-ceiling cabinets. Actors Eduardo de Filippo and Renato Rascel are among past illustrious clients, and if you leaf through the business card samples (the shop's other main speciality) you will find the names of politicians, journalists and actors all printed in different formats and cast in classic typefaces. Vintage Parker pens, smooth leather document holders and 1940s notebooks are among the rare things to be discovered in this treasure trove. They also do repairs so pack that precious fountain pen if it needs fixing.

TRULY PRECIOUS ONE-OFFS
13 Diego Percossi Papi
Via di Sant'Eustachio 16

Diego Percossi Papi has been making bespoke jewelry
for Romans in the know for over 20 years. Indeed his
work is so highly regarded that recently he was made
Cavaliere del Lavoro, one of the highest honours that
Italy can bestow on a working professional. European
aristocrats often drop by his tiny, jewel box of a workshop,
tucked beneath a vine-covered palazzo behind the
Pantheon. What attracts them is his talent for unpicking
family heirlooms and vintage jewelry and combining
them with coloured gemstones, jade, opals and patches of
enamelling. The design follows a long consultation
with the customer, and the results are opulent necklaces
and bracelets filled with personality and imbued with
the style of the Renaissance.

ESPRESSO YOURSELF
14 Il Caffè di Sant'Eustachio
153

JEWEL BOX THEATRE
15 Teatro Valle
Via del Teatro Valle 21

To see inside this small but sumptuous theatre you will
need to buy a ticket for a show, but it is worth it. Built
in 1726, the Teatro Valle is one of Rome's oldest theatres,
with a well-respected calendar of contemporary Italian
and foreign theatre productions as well as the odd
literature festival and musicals. In 1821 it was completely
rebuilt by architect Giuseppe Valadier, the mind behind
the recently reopened, fashionable Casina Valadier (p. 41).
The architect added decorative stucco and bas-reliefs
to the auditorium, with the aim of creating a 'gay and
luminous' ambience. In 1998 a new foyer was built, adding
a more functional entrance to this listed building. Since
1865, the theatre has hosted the most famous actors'
companies and stars, from household names in Italy
like Ermete Zacconi and Anna Magnani to Sarah
Bernhardt. It is much more enchanting than the soulless
city Opera House.

THEATRICAL BASILICA

16 Sant'Andrea della Valle

Piazza Sant'Andrea della Valle

Recently restored to its splendid Baroque beauty, Sant'Andrea della Valle is best known to music cognoscenti as the scene of the first act of *Tosca*. The church was designed by Pier Paolo Olivieri in 1591 and completed Carlo Maderno in 1650; Maderno's dome is the highest in Rome after St Peters. The impressive façade, added in 1665 by Carlo Rainaldi to Maderno's design, features five lower and three upper bays, divided by pairs of projecting columns and crowned by a tympanum. On the upper level, a doorway features the coat of arms of Pope Alexander VII (from the Chigi family). The symmetry is disturbed, however, by a single angel on the left, which has no partner on the right. Apparently, when Alexander VII criticized the sculptor Fancelli's work, he refused to make a second angel. Like many churches in Rome, Sant'Andrea della Valle becomes a pilgrimage site for those visiting cribs during the Christmas season.

WINE EMPORIUM

17 Casa Bleve

152

SPIRALLING BEAUTY

18 Sant'Ivo alla Sapienza

Corso del Rinascimento 40

The stunning shell-shaped dome of the church of Sant'Ivo, crowned by a curvaceous lantern and delicate spiralling tower, was inspired by a series of depictions of the Tower of Babel. Seen from below, it can make the mildest vertigo sufferer feel giddy. Sant'Ivo can be viewed by entering the unassuming door off Corso del Rinascimento. The Palazzo della Sapienza, which is part of the complex, is now the home of the State Archives, founded in 1303 by Pope Boniface VII as Rome's secular university. The church started out as a chapel in the university and was rebuilt in 1642–60 by Borromini and dedicated to St Yves, patron saint of lawyers. The façade has two storeys of arches, which continue along the side walls, flanking a cobblestoned courtyard. The plan of the church is based on an interplay of stars and triangles. Inside, white walls and stucco decoration make it an exquisite example of Roman Baroque. During the summer Sant'Ivo comes alive with a festival of chamber-music concerts.

MASTER AT WORK
19 San Luigi dei Francesi
Piazza di San Luigi dei Francesi 5

Around the corner from the Senate, and just before reaching the Pantheon, is the French national church, built in 1589 by Domenico Fontana and dedicated to Louis IX who led two crusades in the Holy Land. Pass through the imposing façade made of travertine to enter the cool darkness of the interior. It is the Contarelli Chapel, home to three Caravaggio masterpieces, that attracts the steady flow of visitors; insert some coins in the machine to illuminate these canvases, revealing Caravaggio's mastery of light and shadow. *Calling of St Matthew* (1599–1602) shows a gathering of men with St Matthew at the centre, Caravaggio's trademark use of chiaroscuro cutting through the painting like a sword. On the other side of the chapel is *St Matthew and the Angel*. This was the artist's second version of the painting, the first having been deemed unacceptable (it was too radical) by the church officials who commissioned the work. The third painting in the cycle of St Matthew's life, *St Matthew's Martyrdom*, shows a dramatic version of the martyrdom of the saint.

TRADITIONAL HEALING
20 Pontificia Erboristeria
Via del Pozzo delle Cornacchie 26

This herbalist shop first opened in 1780 and is one of the 'historical shops of Rome'. After two centuries of commercial activity it was shut down in 1980, but, luckily, in 1997 it reopened under new management. The products on sale are the result of a long history of herbal medicine as practised by religious monastic orders. Many of the remedies available today follow the original recipes.

SICILIAN CHIC
21 Trattoria
147

INTELLIGENT TOYS
22 Città del Sole
165

DESIGNER DRINKING
23 Riccioli Cafe
155

CLEVERLY CUT CLOTHES
24 Tombolini
Via della Maddalena 31–38

Lovers of camel cashmere coats, smart suits and crisp white shirts will find it hard not to be tempted in Tombolini, the flagship store of this classic Italian label, which keeps its contemporary edge thanks to great cuts and a tradition of craftsmanship in textiles. The spacious environment in Via della Maddalena sells menswear and womenswear as well as a selection of shoes and leather accessories. Eugenio Tombolini started the label in the 1960s after an apprenticeship as a tailor. Tombolini's headquarters are in Urbisaglia, in the Macerata region, famous as a textile manufacturing centre; indeed, the group also produces and distributes Thierry Mugler and Romeo Gigli. The company is still in the family, with daughter Fiorella Tombolini at its helm distributing the brand worldwide.

WELL SUITED
25 Davide Cenci
173

PEDESTRIAN HEAVEN
26 Piazza di San Lorenzo in Lucina
• Bar Vitti Centro, no. 33
• Profumeria Materozzoli, no. 5
• Spada, no. 20
• Bonpoint, no. 25
• Yien, Via di Campo Marzio 33

Away from the frenzy of Via del Corso, step into Piazza di San Lorenzo in Lucina and you are transported back into an idealized version of what city life must have been like a couple of hundred years ago. Nannies push prams, *signore* walk their poodles and chic cyclists dismount for an afternoon *gelato*. From Bar Vitti, the constant waft of freshly baked pastries – puff-pastry parcels with ricotta cheese and chocolate are the speciality – is heady. On the square, the perfumery Materozzoli is where to stock up on Acqua di Parma, while Spada is a good choice for those aspiring to the classic 'Roman gentleman' look. Here, Massimo Barcaroli sells ties of every hue and type of fabric. Next door is Bonpoint, a rather expensive children's shop with hand-stitched linen dresses and crocheted hats. Further up, in Via di Campo Marzio, Yien has beaded sandals, linen embroidered kaftans, funky sunglasses and leather goods.

In a city where ice-cream making is almost an art form, there is always going to be a lively debate about which offers the best. Giolitti's reputation as the most authentic is justified by its long history and use of simple, fresh ingredients. Started in 1890 by Giuseppe and Bernardina Giolitti, it evolved from a humble *latteria* (a dairy shop for milk and butter) into today's meeting point for families on their daily *passeggiata*. Over the years, the Giolitti family has opened other parlours in the city, but the original one, with its turn-of-the-20th-century décor and faded charm, remains a firm favourite. The cups are Giolitti's main claim to fame, especially the zabaione, nougat and chocolate *Coppa Olimpica*, a towering concoction created to commemorate the 1960 Olympic Games.

Daniele Costantini certainly drew inspiration from his art studies for the décor of Boccondivino, a cool ambience where modern classics like faux zebra-covered Bertoia chairs blend with original De Chirico prints or contemporary Italian paintings. Housed in a 16th-century palazzo facing the faded blue Santa Maria in Campo Marzio, this could easily be just another tourist trap along the Pantheon route, yet for over ten years the restaurant has been serving well-executed fare at mid-range prices. Specialities include lentil soup, black squid-ink pasta with clams and asparagus, duck with juniper and salmon tartare.

29 Obika
Via dei Prefetti 26a

Mozzarella connoisseurs flock en masse to Obika, a recently opened mozzarella bar in the centre of Rome. Conceived mainly as a stopover for lunch, Obika offers three varieties of mozzarella – *Casertana*, *Salernitana* and *Pontina* – produced around Naples and delivered daily at 8 a.m. Among the several delicacies on the menu, firm favourites are the hand-cut mozzarella from the Campania, served with anchovies and caper flowers, and a fiordilatte cheese from Salento combined with onion chutney. Obika means 'here it is' in Neapolitan dialect, but here it has been spelt to sound similar to Japanese. Indeed, sushi bars are the inspiration behind Obika, with its circular counter, from which the dishes are quickly assembled, stools and see-through perspex containers for the organic salads, cheeses and hams. Designed by rising young Roman architects Labics, Obika cleverly blends stark modernism with typical Roman touches, such as the airy archways in the dining room at the back. In the evening, Obika evolves into a sophisticated eaterie, with pasta dishes reinforcing the lunch menu and a carefully selected Italian wine list. A brainchild of Silvio Ursini, an executive at Bulgari, Obika has rapidly become one of the city's favourite meeting points for young professionals, fashion folk and gourmets, who thrive in the buzzing atmosphere and friendly service, and worship the divine cheese. Future plans include expansion in other European cities.

FABRIC OF SOCIETY
30 Passamanerie Crocianelli
Vie dei Prefetti 37–40

Haberdasheries have been selling *passamanerie* (lengths of ribbon, braided cord and colourful tassels used as trimmings for furnishings) in Rome for centuries. This 100-year-old, listed shop is a treasure trove for anyone remotely interested in home decoration. All the trimmings are arranged by colour and placed in original wood cabinets that line the walls of the shop. Quaint needlepoint pillows and embroidery kits are also on sale. Bargains can be found by rummaging in the baskets of leftover stock.

OLD HAUNT
31 La Campana

PICASSO INSPIRED
32 Il desiderio preso per la coda
Vicolo della Palomba 23

Named after a piece of avant-garde theatre by Picasso, Il desiderio preso per la coda (the desire caught by the tail) has a subtle but noticeable presence in this little-known alleyway behind Piazza Navona. The small *enoteca* has been serving good, unfussy Tuscan-inspired food for over a decade, such as *pappa al pomodoro* (bread and tomato soup), as well as their own *farfalle picassiane*, pasta tossed with olives, pine nuts, tomatoes and parmesan shavings. The real treat, however, is to dine amidst the small collection of Italian Arte Povera, which is owned by artist and collector Anna Pocchiari, the wife of the restaurateur Corrado Parisi.

CAPSULE COLLECTION
33 Dulce Vidoza
Via dell'Orso 58

Dulce Vidoza may sound like the name of a heroine in a Gabriel García Márquez novel, but it is the real name of the Venezuelan designer who owns this small but perfectly formed shop. Designed by her husband, the well-known Roman architect Massimo D'Alessandro, the space functions as a sleek container to a multicoloured capsule collection. All the items are created from Indian silks, crisp linens or mid-20th-century vintage fabrics. Delicate tea dresses, Nehru collared shirts and 1950s swing skirts are among the styles favoured by Dulce Vidoza. Finding the right size can sometimes be a problem as the garments are only made so long as the precious fabric lasts.

TRADITIONAL TRATTORIA
34 Da Settimio all'Arancio
Via dell'Arancio 50–52
• L'Arancio d'Oro, Via di Monte d'Oro 17
• Al Piccolo Arancio, Vicolo Scanderberg 112

Journalists and politicians have been coming to Settimio for over twenty-five years, attracted by the informal atmosphere and late-night closing times, so it's worth booking in advance. Waiters bustle around and the menu is reassuringly traditional, with house specials like *ravioli all'arancia* (stuffed with ricotta cheese and oranges), and there is always a good selection of fresh fish. On summer evenings, the outside seating area offers respite from the heat and becomes the setting for fellow diners to strike up conversation. The establishment is so popular that two other Arancio-style restaurants – L'Arancio d'Oro and Al Piccolo Arancio – have recently opened. Brothers Luciano, Lino, Luigi and Mara run this small gastronomic empire under the attentive eye of their father, Settimio, the original founder.

FAIRYTALE COUTURE
35 Sorelle Fontana

SEA-THEMED FOOD
36 Reef
Piazza Augusto Imperatore 42–48

Twins Marco and Gianluigi Giammetta, former pupils of Massimiliano Fuksas, are the architects behind Reef, a sea-themed restaurant on the corner of Piazza Augusto Imperatore. In contrast to the 1930s Fascist-style exterior, the interiors are decisively high tech, with oxidized iron, steel cables and cloudy green glass used throughout. The main dining area is conceived as the deck of a ship and has a glass floor below which is sand and water with pieces of broken glass floating on top, giving the surface a wind-rippled effect. On the walls, oversized photographs of fish reinforce the idea that you are viewing the sea world from the portholes of a ship. From the back-lit emerald green bar you can spot the chefs in the open-plan kitchen scurrying to and fro while preparing dishes. A decked patio outside offers cool and sheltered alfresco dining.

SENSORY OVERLOAD
39 L' Olfattorio Bar à Parfums
Via di Ripetta 34

Fancy a flute of Mûre et Musc, or a rose cocktail by Les Parfums de Rosine? The suggestion that you can stimulate your nose in the same way that champagne titillates the taste buds is the idea behind L'Olfattorio Bar à Parfums, a perfume bar opened in 2002 by husband-and-wife team Giovanni Gaidano and Renata De Rossi. Designed as a clinically white showroom, the bar sells luxury brands such as L'Artisan Parfumeur, Diptyque, Les Parfums de Rosine, Coudray and Compagnie de Provence with wit and elegance. Customers are invited to experience olfactory therapy, sniffing at the American Bar counter goblets of eau de parfume and eau de toilette. Jean Paul Guerlain defined perfume as the most overwhelming form of memory, and so the Gaidanos play with the effect that scents such as rosemary and ylang ylang can have on our psyche.

QUIRKY TROVES
40 Mario Squatriti Restauri Artistici
Via di Ripetta 29

The window displays of Mario Squatriti Restauri Artistici look like the set of a Hammer horror film. In fact, there is a sense of macabre about the whole shop: distressed antique dolls' heads, limbs and other body parts are stacked up in piles and covered with cobwebs. Mario Squatriti is mainly a restorer of fine Italian ceramics but he also specializes in 18th- and 19th-century antiques. Vintage dolls are his passion, which he carefully returns to past glory, and there are theatrical antics in the way he displays his bizarre bric-à-brac.

Miss Sixty may be an international brand, but it began as a Roman success story. Vicky Hassan created his streetwear empire in the mid-1980s and has gone on to produce labels Energie, Killah, Sixty, RefrigiWear and Ayor. His taste for sexy, funky designs has turned Miss Sixty into a cult label among models and pop celebrities who love the slim-fit jeans, day-glow plastic sandals and retro bags. The original flagship store in Via del Corso has been refitted by architects Studio 63 as part of a strategy for worldwide expansion. The feel is that of a 1960s airport lounge-meets-boudoir, with Verner Panton chairs, red velvet curtains, fluffy carpets and white-lacquered, space age-style display cabinets. The frivolous and kitsch interiors reflect the youthful feel of the brand.

Anyone who aspires to add some ancient Roman style to their home should consider a visit to Maurizio Grossi's shop in Via Margutta. Inside, marble obelisks are lined up with reproductions of Roman sculptures. Mosaics depicting ancient Greek and Roman scenes can be specially designed and shipped abroad. Clients include the king of Morocco, who commissioned Grossi to create three large cast-iron tables encased with precious marble mosaics. For smaller gifts, the deceptively real-looking figs of marble, and eggs carved out of semi-precious stones make for an original memento. Attention is given to the craftmanship and the quality of different tones, from numidian marble to onyx and antique imperial red and black marble.

47 Gente

Via del Babuino 80–82

Gente is the place where many a Roman fashionista, model or *perbene* (well-to-do) shopper goes for their major fashion fix. Over the years it has expanded to two other shops in the centre of Rome, but this one, located in the boutique heaven of Via del Babuino, is the original, and still offers the best selection. Over two floors, labels from Italy and elsewhere cram the rails: Prada, Helmut Lang, Gucci, Romeo Gigli and Anna Sui are just some of the names. Upstairs, there is a well-stocked menswear selection as well as an eveningwear department with grown-up gown collections by John Galliano, Jil Sanders and Ann Demeulemeester. An accessories section with funky patchwork-style bags from Marni and strappy sandals from Prada ensures gratifying retail relief on every visit.

NATIONAL CHIC
48 Costume National

171

PALATIAL EXPERIENCE
49 Palazzetto at the International Wine Academy

120

SHOE FETISH
50 Dal Cò

168

WINE AND FOOD
51 L'Enoteca Antica

Via della Croce 76b

As inscription on several of the wine amphorae that line the shelves reminds visitors that this small and always packed wine bar has been trading in *vini e olii* (wines and oils) since 1726. Like most of the city's grocery stores of that period, it also sold soap, coal, whisky and cognac. Transformed into an *enoteca* twenty years ago, the front area now functions as a wine shop filled to the rafters with excellent French and Italian wines and liquors. In one corner, a turn-of-the-20th-century marble counter is where you get light snacks from the bar's menu. Good, simple Roman favourites like *frittata di patate* (potato omelette), *mozzarella di bufala* (buffalo milk mozzarella)

and a cold salad of beans and celery are served with a wide selection of wines by the glass. In the back room a sit-down restaurant offers pasta and meat dishes such as *vitello tonnato* (veal in a tuna and mayonnaise sauce) at reasonable prices.

TOOLS FOR COOKS
52 C.U.C.I.N.A

167

FITS LIKE A GLOVE
53 Sermoneta

172

DELUXE DESIGNS
54 Bulgari

170

VERY VALENTINO
55 Valentino

175

SALADS AND SNACKS
56 Shaki Wine Bar

Via Mario de' Fiori 29a

Not content with heading the Sermoneta dynasty, merchants of the finest gloves in Rome (p. 172), Manuela Sermoneta has expanded into hospitality with this busy and bustling wine bar just off Via Condotti. Named after her children, Shaki is a continuation of the homeware brand that Sermoneta set up in nearby Piazza di Spagna: it sells everything, from pottery to preserves. The wine bar prides itself on its own-baked bread, generously sized salads and wide selection of Italian wine labels. The décor basks in blonde wood panelling and cube-shaped seating units.

PAST MEMORIES
57 Caffè Greco

153

SUPERIOR SOCKS
58 Schostal

169

OLD WORLD CHIC
59 Battistoni

168

Lovers of Italian cinema might recall Alberto Sordi's 1973 comedy *Polvere di Stelle* in which he and his wife, played by Monica Vitti, are two poverty-stricken music hall performers struggling to get a break in post-war Italy. One of the scenes was filmed in the Galleria Colonna, an Art Déco–style arcade built in 1922. When the Galleria reopened to the public in 2003, after a long period of restoration, it was named in Sordi's honour by Rome's mayor, film fan Walter Veltroni. New mosaic floors now adorn the Galleria, while the ceiling stucco decorations have been restored to their former glory. The Galleria has swiftly become a backdrop to many Romans' afternoon *passeggiata*. The large Feltrinelli bookstore is worth a visit and the cafés under the arcades are a pleasant place to stop, especially the central one, which features a menu overseen by chef and restaurateur Alberto Ciarla.

The Giorgio de Chirico house-museum opened to the public in November 1998, the 20th anniversary of the artist's death. The townhouse occupies the three upper floors of the historic 17th-century Palazzetto dei Borgognoni, situated just off the Spanish Steps. Bought in 1947, the artist and his wife, Isabella Pakzswer Far, lived here from 1948. The building's façade faces Piazza di Spagna where it overlooks Bernini's fountain. At the back there are views of Trinità dei Monti and Villa Medici, the gardens of which feature in a number of De Chirico's romantic and historical paintings. The artist's studio is located at the top of the house. A few of the plaster models that De Chirico used are scattered around the studio in an attempt to re-create the working atmosphere of the Metaphysical painter. The studio library contains a large collection of art books, which touch upon the themes and key artistic periods that he studied. Furnished during the 1950s, both the rooms and the hanging of the paintings have been kept as they were originally arranged, although the Foundation rotates its collection of some sixty artworks. Nearby is the Roman residence of the English poet John Keats, a pale pink building that is now the Keats–Shelley Memorial House. Keats died here in 1821 of consumption, just four months after his arrival in Italy; he is buried in the Protestant cemetery in Testaccio (p. 89). The residence was bought in 1906, thanks to the efforts of a group of American and English poets. Included in the amazing collection is the locket that Elizabeth Barrett Browning gave to Robert Browning.

Although Italy, and Rome in particular, is awash with shoe shops, there is always space for more. Fausto Santini can justifiably claim to be one of the most loved shoe designers in the city. It's easy to see why: organic shapes, low heels and soft leathers are turned into simple but fashionable classics that live well beyond the season's diktats. All over the store are tiny handwritten signs bidding the shopper 'Please Touch'; the feel of the leather bags and shoes is a reward in itself. For those who are die-hard fans, don't forget to visit Fausto Santini's outlet store in Via Cavour, just down from Santa Maria Maggiore, where last season's collections are sold at a fraction of the price.

Italians have a well-known disposition for luxury and well-crafted objects, so it is hardly surprising that Eleuteri ranks as a firm favourite gift shop among the politicians of the nearby Montecitorio (parliament). This silverware and jewelry shop offers 20th-century Art-Nouveau jewelry as well as colourful 1940s gold and pieces set with precious stones. Contemporary pieces are by Boucheron, Bulgari and Cartier. The large, opulent silver trays are often of English origin.

FANCY FOOTWEAR
66 Herzel
Via di Propaganda 14

Herzel de Bach's unashamedly sexy shoes have been a hit among ladies who lunch since he opened his shop behind the Spanish Steps twenty-five years ago. Following the success of his first boutique, another one at nearby Via del Babuino 123 soon followed. A word-of-mouth brand that does not advertise and can only be found in Rome, Herzel's speciality is the use of soft leathers dyed in glittering silvers and golds, as well as pastel colours. High heels and a price tag to match make a pair of Herzel shoes a status symbol.

AN ECCENTRIC GUESTHOUSE
67 Casa Howard

PRETTY CHILDREN'S WEAR
68 Lavori Artigianali Femminili
Via di Capo le Case 6

In a world saturated by chains, it is refreshing to find a shop selling handmade and one-off children's clothes. The items are so pretty that just a glimpse at the old-fashioned window display could distract mothers from their Prada account to invest in a wardrobe for their offspring. Lavori Artigianali Femminili has embroidered household linens, exquisitely embroidered baby clothes and smocked christening dresses. These are precious clothes for special occasions, but they are worth the expense.

COMFORT FOOD
69 Colline Emiliane
Via degli Avignonesi 22

Those nostalgic for north Italian fare come to this restaurant to sample dishes like *tortellini in brodo* (tortellini in broth), *bolliti* (boiled meat) and pumpkin-stuffed pasta. The wooden décor is reassuringly rustic; this place is about satisfying the stomach rather than the eye. The restaurant has been here since 1931 when Bologna-born Mario Falchieri opened an establishment that focused on the cuisine of the Emilia region. It was bought by the Latini family in 1967, who still run it today. Since then nothing has changed, whether it is the menu or the discreet service offered by white-jacketed waiters.

BAROQUE SPLENDOUR
70 Galleria Nazionale d'Arte Antica di Palazzo Barberini
Via delle Quattro Fontane 13

The idea of entering the home of one of Rome's grandest aristocratic families is just one of the many charms of the Barberini Gallery. Past the Bernini fountain *Il Tritone* in Piazza Barberini and up the hill to Via delle Quattro Fontane stands the extravagant 17th-century Palazzo Barberini, begun by Carlo Maderno and completed by rival architects Borromini and Bernini for Maffeo Barberini, Pope Urban VIII. The style is Roman Baroque at its peak, with staircases, arches and a great central portico built to glorify the pomp and circumstance of the Barberini family's world. The stunning frescoed ceiling in the main hall is by Pietro da Cortona and dates back to 1633. Renamed the Galleria Nazionale d'Arte Antica when the palace was sold to the Italian state, the museum is packed with masterpieces, some from the original Barberini collection and others from the Corsini Palace in Trastevere. Raphael's portrait of his supposed mistress, *La Fornarina*, is one of the most popular pieces on display, but there is also a Filippo Lippi *Madonna and Child* and Tintoretto's *Christ and the Adulteress* as well as paintings by Caravaggio, Titian and El Greco.

STYLISH SNACKS
71 Moma
Via di San Basilio 42–43

Perhaps inspired by the uncompromisingly contemporary décor of the nearby Aleph Hotel (p. 128), the Moma wine bar and restaurant is another little oasis of uncluttered design in an area otherwise filled with Baroque excess. While the name is a nod to New York's Museum of Modern Art, it also is a reference to the expression in Roman dialect, '*Mò magnamo*', 'now we eat'. Open for breakfast with freshly baked croissants, at lunchtime the bar is besieged by elegantly suited employees from the nearby ministries and embassies. Snacks that include deep-fried mozzarella, anchovy croutons and freshly made fruit salads can be eaten perched on stools or at the bar. Upstairs, a small dining hall caters for those preferring a three-course lunch or dinner. The menu is modern Italian – seared tuna, spaghetti with clams and asparagus – and so is the extensive wine list, which can be ordered by the glass.

A RITZ IN ROME

72 Tearooms at Saint Regis Grand Hotel

Via Vittorio Emanuele Orlando 3

The opulence of the Saint Regis Grand might not appeal to everyone, with its columned reception room, Murano glass chandeliers, frescoes and Empire and Regency-style furniture. It was opened by Cesar Ritz in 1894 as Le Grand, one of Rome's first deluxe hotels. Reopened in 1999 after a major facelift, the hotel's luxurious facilities are favoured by heads of state, politicians and executives. For those who only want to dip into this money-dripping atmosphere, afternoon tea is the perfect occasion. Like its famous sister hotel, the Ritz in London, it does know how to present a fine spread for tea. You might find the harp music in the lounge a touch annoying, but there is nothing that cannot be digested when sampling delicious Italian patisserie, finger sandwiches and petit fours, all served on grand silver dishes.

SEVENTH HEAVEN

73 Aleph Hotel

74 Santa Maria della Vittoria
Via XX Settembre 17

A delightful semi-hidden church off Via XX Settembre, Santa Maria della Vittoria should be visited to see Bernini's magnificent Cornaro Chapel. Built between 1645 and 1652, the chapel was designed as a theatre: eight members of the Venetian Cornaro family are represented as if watching the sacred scene *The Ecstasy of St Theresa* in the niche of the altar. The statue of St Theresa, portrayed by Bernini with eyes half closed and open mouthed, is alarmingly realistic. While Victorians were shocked by the sensuality of the piece, others find it saintly and inspired. The angel drawing the dart away from the saint's sinking body is framed by an explosion of golden rays, a device that Bernini used later in St Peter's.

75 Sant'Isidoro
Via degli Artisti 41

To gain entrance to this small Baroque masterpiece just keep buzzing at the gates of the little church off Via Vittorio Veneto; your patience will eventually be rewarded and staff from the Irish Church (there are now only a few priests who actually live here) will let you in. Recently restored, Sant'Isidoro's main attraction is the Da Sylva Chapel, designed by Bernini in 1660. The over-painting from past restorations has finally been removed; it included some horrible bronze cover-ups that were applied to the naked figures of Truth and Charity in the 18th century.

Facing the presidential palace, the Scuderie of Il Quirinale, which was named after the hill on which it is perched, were the palace's coach houses and stables until 1938. In 1999 architect Gae Aulenti gutted the whole space and transformed it into a magnificent 3000-square-metre cultural venue that plays host to photographic, modern-art and travelling exhibitions. The exquisitely restrained interior restoration features vaulted ceilings and airy rooms all decorated in hues of Rome's trademark travertine. The panoramic view of the city, from the back exit glass stairway, is among the many, often surprising assets of Le Scuderie. Don't miss the bookstore on the ground floor, with its extensive selection of art books, mostly in Italian.

The glorious days of *la dolce vita* may never come again, but there is a definite revival going on along Via Vittorio Veneto, with many establishments along this famous street undergoing a revamp, including Café de Paris. Upstairs in the Sala degli Angeli tea room, the atmosphere is clubby and secluded, with deep red décor and cute golden angels. Tea is becoming increasingly popular in Rome, the idea being to serve pastries with a fine selection of Darjeeling, Ceylon Pekoe, Formosa Fancy Oolong and several Japanese green teas, as well as high cocoa content chocolate like the Venezuelan Chuao, which has a pleasantly bitter flavour, and Toscano White, flavoured with vanilla.

81 Doney
Via Vittorio Veneto 125

Richard Burton, Burt Lancaster and Ava Gardner were all snapped by paparazzi here during the heady days of the 1950s and 1960s, but in 2000 the bar was acquired by the Westin Excelsior Hotel next door. 'Hip, hot and happy' is how the management describes the new Doney. The black and red furnishing, geometrically clad mannequins, candles and chandeliers might be teetering on the verge of overkill, but the club makes a refreshing change from the much blander examples along the same street. On the pavement, the comfy sofas and wrought-iron tables provide a small oasis of calm, protected from the hustle and bustle of traffic by red tent-like structures. From here you can admire the quarter, which is of architectural interest. Created between the late 1800s and the early 1900s by the Boncompagni Ludovisi princes, it is an early example of real estate speculation. The princes divided the land belonging to their 17th-century villa into lots, paving the way for the construction of several distinguished-looking buildings, including Villa Margherita, today home to the American Embassy.

PLEASING PIZZERIA

82 San Marco
Via Sardegna 38d

Cooly set in a spacious double area with a decked patio dining area outside, San Marco, so-called because the owners used to run a pizzeria of the same name, belongs to the Gusto (p. 144) school of thought: make top-quality Italian food work within a pleasingly designed environment. The main space features several decorative themes: the front room has long cherrywood tables, hanging lights and murals inscribed with quotes from Andy Warhol, while at the back it is rustic with an edge – trattoria-style chairs blend in with salvaged grocery cabinets. Cleverly packaged own-brand San Marco oils and wines line the floor-to-ceiling shelves. Next door, huge chalk walls are scribbled with recipes, while anecdotes and drawings of food frame the bar area. San Marco calls itself a wine bar, grill, restaurant and pizzeria, which means that you can use it pretty much as you like. Customers include a few tourists (after all, we are not far from the Via Vittorio Veneto strip) and large parties on a night out.

FAMILY HEIRLOOMS
83 Galleria Borghese
Piazzale del Museo Borghese 5

Set in the green oasis of Villa Borghese, also home to Rome's much improved zoo, the Galleria Borghese is an occasion to peek into the splendours of what has been described as the finest non-royal private collection in the world. Opened in 1998 after being shut for many years, the gallery houses a remarkable and well-displayed collection of masterpieces. Antonio Canova's sculpture of *Paolina Borghese* (Napoleon Bonaparte's sister) as Venus is a triumph of neoclassicism, and Bernini's *David*, executed when the sculptor was only twenty-five years old, represented a revolution in art – it was designed with multiple viewing points in mind. Paintings by Caravaggio and Raphael are just some of the other treasures to be discovered in these sumptuously decorated rooms. Visits are limited to two hours and advance booking is essential.

CHARMING TOWN LODGE
84 Casina Valadier, Villa Borghese
Piazza Bucarest

Designed by architect Giuseppe Valadier between 1816 and 1837, the Casina is a neoclassical lodge set on the border of the Pincio park inside Villa Borghese. With its mesmerizing views of the north side of Rome, it was originally conceived as a meeting point for the city's chattering classes (the idea was to make it into a French-style bistro), but its location was considered a touch remote by those artists who preferred the cafés around Piazza del Popolo. It was only during the First World War that the Casina really came in its own – Mahatma Ghandi, Richard Strauss and King Farouk were among its illustrious visitors. Then, in the 1980s, Casina Valadier became the favourite spot of the capital's media and political brigade to power-lunch. Lengthy restoration work followed in the 1990s, and when it reopened in the summer of 2004, with a new look by architects Cesareni e Marsaglia and a menu devised by Antonio Sciullo, previously the chef at Hotel Byron, the beautiful and the powerful started to flock here en masse. Today, whether you dine on the terrace or choose the cafeteria in the gardens, you will experience only the very best Mediterranean produce and first-rate service, signalling a return to former glory of one of the city's most fascinating locations.

NEW ADDITION
85 MAXXI
Via Guido Reni 10

It may not be completed until 2006, but Rome's new contemporary art and architecture centre has already been the subject of more column inches than any other recent cultural initiative in the city, which is hardly surprising since the Museum of Art for the XXI Century, or MAXXI as it is known, has been designed by the celebrated architect Zaha Hadid. Hadid's project is one of several recent high-profile commissions in Rome, which include Renzo Piano's Auditorium (see next page) and Odile Decq's Macro Museum. In a city that was reluctant to admit new designs, these projects signal the start of a new era, one that will put Rome firmly on the map for contemporary public architecture. Hadid's two-storey, 26,000-square-metre scheme for MAXXI offers a flexible space for exhibitions and live events. During construction, exhibitions are being held in a loft-style space that has been converted from the old army barracks.

CULTURAL CENTRE
86 Macro
Via Reggio Emilia 54

Formerly an early 20th-century Peroni brewery, Macro, designed by French architect Odile Decq, opened in 2002 as Rome's first museum dedicated to contemporary art. Tony Oursler, Cecily Brown and Andreas Gursky are among the artists to have showcased here. The artworks blend with the high-tech, luminous architecture. Skylights, see-through glass lifts and a couple of bridges that connect the two original buildings lend the environment an industrial feel – the furniture and lighting were designed by Decq and produced by Poltrona Frau and Luceplan. The permanent collection is dedicated to Italian art of the 1960s. A guided tour includes pieces by the Scuola di Piazza del Popolo, Tano Festa, Mario Schifano and Titina Maselli, and by Arte Povera members Mario Ceroli and Pino Pascali, as well as by Piero Pizzi Cannella, Gianni Dessì and Bruno Ceccobelli, a group that sprang up in the 1980s in the San Lorenzo area and is now known as the Nuova Scuola Romana. Planned for 2005 is a new wing by Decq, featuring a roof terrace, garden and galleries.

COUNTRY STYLE IN THE CITY
87 Baba
146

88 Auditorium Parco della Musica

Viale Pietro de Coubertin 30

Three glistening scarab-shaped structures are the unlikely symbols of Rome's recent architectural renaissance. The Auditorium, designed by Genoa's most fêted son, Renzo Piano, is wedged between the 1960s Olympic village and the busy Corso Francia flyover, just two kilometres from central Piazza del Popolo. Finally providing the city with a proper venue for classical music, this is where the orchestra of Rome, the National Academy of Santa Cecilia, has taken up residence. Conceived as a 'park of music', the Auditorium comprises three music halls, each specifically 'tuned' for a different type of performance. With meticulous attention to the acoustics, Piano teamed up with specialists at Müller-BBM of Munich to create a hall seating 700 people, suitable for chamber music and other small concerts, a medium-sized hall seating 1200 for symphonic music and ballet, and a larger one accommodating 2700 for opera and modern music. Outside, the 3000-seat capacity of the Cavea recalls the Greco-Roman tradition of amphitheatres. The airy foyer connecting the different halls features giant neon artworks by Maurizio Nannucci, each spelling out music-inspired quotes from artists as varied as Haydn, Lennon and Kandinsky and a collection of twelve pieces by Sebastian Matta, part of the Auditorium's growing art collection. On a smaller scale, the elegant and lush Red restaurant serves Mediterranean-inspired food; later in the evening resident DJ Fabio Ottaviani directs a series of popular club nights, with Good Grooves on Fridays. Next door, the Note Book bookstore stocks an international selection of art and design books as well as a large CD selection. Piano won the competition to design the Auditorium nearly ten years ago. However, when construction work began, the ruins of a 4th-century BC villa were unearthed. Building was halted and a two-year excavation ensued, revealing a wealth of artefacts and structural walls, which are now enclosed in an archaeological area and museum.

Campo de' Fiori
Piazza Navona

Until the 1970s, Campo de' Fiori was a centre of thievery and drug dealing, with the police reluctant to intervene. How times change. But Campo de' Fiori has retained its authentic Roman flavour – a mix of theatre and chaos, riotous colour and beauty. The site of one the city's oldest fruit and vegetable markets, it is the only square in Catholic Rome without a church. In its place stands the statue of Giordano Bruno, the heretic burnt at the stake in 1600. The square built up a grim reputation as the venue for executions. Today, the recently restored pastel-hued, medieval palazzi that surround it are punctuated by family-run grocery stores, flower stalls, ice-cream emporiums and bakeries selling slices of warm pizza.

Lounging over a cappuccino in a small outdoor café while watching market sellers bellow their offerings is arguably the best way to absorb the neighbourhood's spirit. While by day the square goes about its bustling, odoriferous business, from early evening onwards it becomes a favourite hang-out, where the bars and pizzerie cater to a crowd of youthful, insomniac revellers. The area's rowdy reputation is well rooted in the past – just behind the Campo is Largo del Pallaro, where Julius Caesar was stabbed to death in 44 BC.

In serene contrast, Piazza Farnese, seat of the French Embassy, is only a block away. From there you can drift into beautiful, lamp-lit Via Giulia (p. 48), with its wondrous vine-clad arch designed by Michelangelo. All around, the dark, cobbled alleyways carry the names of the artisans who had workshops here during medieval times. Via dei Cappellari (the hat makers' street), Via dei Giubbonari (the jacket makers' street) and Via dei Chiavari (the locksmiths' street) provide clues to the past, but today they are more likely to house boutiques selling everything from antiques to handmade shoes, as well as the requisite art galleries and wine bars.

Across the Corso Vittorio Emanuele is the area around Piazza Navona. Here the atmosphere is more genteel: the attractive streets of Via del Governo Vecchio (p. 59) and Via dei Coronari are some of the city's most covetable addresses. *Enoteca* bars, vintage shops and chic boutiques like L'una e L'altra (p. 164) cater to the affluent residents, while the Pace triangle, comprising Bar della Pace (p. 151), Bar del Fico (p. 155) and Bramante, is the one of Rome's most fashionable drinking spots. Tourist-thronged Piazza Navona (p. 60) struggles to combine the beauty of its Baroque architecture with the incongruous presence of stall vendors selling cheap football merchandise, but Borromini's extravagant Sant'Agnese in Agone, the opulent Palazzo Pamphilj, now the Brazilian Embassy, and the Fontana dei Quattro Fiumi by Bernini are gems not to be overlooked.

1 Via Giulia

Despite the cars that run through it, this beautiful 16th-century cobblestoned street makes for a delightful paved promenade any time of the day or evening. Flanked by antiques shops and costume-jewelry boutiques, its centrepiece is probably the Palazzo Farnese, partly designed by Michelangelo, today the seat of the French Embassy. Named after its creator, Pope Julius II, Via Giulia was devised as part of his master plan to create a new route to St Peter's, to have been carried out by Bramante but which foundered when funds ran out; the pope died before it was completed. Start at the top of Via Giulia at San Giovanni dei Fiorentini and stroll towards the end, just where it meets Ponte Sisto, the bridge that crosses the Tiber into Trastevere.

A RAW APPROACH
2 Crudo

HOUSE PROUD
3 Spazio Sette

FUNKY WARES
4 Angelo di Nepi
Via dei Giubbonari 28

Angelo di Nepi has several boutiques scattered throughout town, and each reflects the understated elegance with which he is associated. His trademark is a red chilli, symbolic of a 'made in Italy' pedigree, but his talent lies in transforming vividly coloured silks, cottons and linens into refined, classic dresses, trousers and shirts. Over the past twenty years, Di Nepi has established a faithful clientele of well-heeled Roman women who adore his unassuming but charming pieces. All his shops are designed by Victor Raccah and feature a strong juxtaposition of old and new, exemplified by Roman-style mosaics cast into cement floors, and 1950s Bohemian crystal chandeliers with bespoke coloured lamps.

SHOP AND DINE
5 Roscioli

PRIVATE VIEW
6 Palazzo Spada
Piazza Capo di Ferro 13

Wander into the delightfully irregular Piazza della Quercia, where a large oak tree stands amid the ochre-tinted palazzi, and you will think that you have stepped into a scene in 16th-century Rome. Designed in 1550 by Giulio Mazzoni, Palazzo Spada is a triumph of frivolous stucco decoration, an early anticipation of Baroque excess, which contrasts with the austerity of nearby Palazzo Farnese. The most unusual feature of this palazzo, now the seat of the Italian State Council, is Borromini's trompe-l'oeil perspective (1652–53), which can be seen from the courtyard. The artworks on display in the four-room gallery come from Cardinal Bernardino Spada's small but beautifully formed collection, and include a number of 16th- and 17th-century paintings and fine Roman sculptures. Titian, Guercino, Annibale Carracci, Guido Reni and Gaspar Dughet are among the artists on display.

CAPPUCCINO CENTRAL
7 Bar Farnese
Piazza Farnese 106–107

Affluent locals, entranced tourists and the odd dog walker are among those who enjoy Bar Farnese's exceptional location, perched on the corner of the piazza of the same name and facing one of the finest Renaissance palaces in Rome. The rows of tables spilling into Via dei Baullari are always packed, especially during sunny weekend mornings, but while you are waiting you can always buy the papers (there is a good selection of international titles available) at the next door news stand. Breakfast is traditionally Italian, with *cornetti* filled with jam, cream or chocolate, while *tramezzini*, triangular sandwiches, make a perfect lunchtime snack.

PRETTY PURCHASES
8 Baullà
Via dei Baullari 37

Everything in Baullà's cramped premises has a story to tell, from the silk travel sheets sourced in Cambodia to the 1950s-style Vietnamese print fashioned into a one-off skirt. The textiles of the Far East are certainly an inspiration, so too are the crafts of rural northern Italy: the shop sells stacks of the soft velvet slippers produced in the Veneto region and traditionally worn at home or during Carnival, which you can get in every colour combination possible, even in soft suede. From natty wicker bags with pink handles to linen hats and caps in soft wool, Baullà is a treasure trove for quirky, individual pieces.

MELODIOUS MEALS
9 Ditirambo
Piazza della Cancelleria 74–75

Amid the disappointing restaurants in the Campo de' Fiori area, Ditirambo is a pleasant surprise. Named after a chant in honour of Dionysus, the restaurant was founded by Dado, a wine merchant, Beatrice, an antiques dealer, Luca, a marketing manager and Marco, an actor. The ingredients are all sourced from farms and small producers across Italy. It is a pleasantly small establishment, which gets packed with Romans who enjoy their creative modern Italian cooking, so it is worth booking in advance. Homemade pasta is served with tasty, imaginative sauces like chestnuts or courgette flowers. Vegetarians are well catered for with dishes such as stuffed radicchio parcels or pumpkin strudel. Desserts, which include tarte tatin with chocolate sauce and *millefoglie* with muscat-flavoured zabaione, are truly scrumptious.

10 La Libreria del Viaggiatore
Via del Pellegrino 78

The shelves at Bruno Boschin's well-stocked travel bookstore positively groan with information and publications about other cultures in every corner of the globe. The tiny shop is packed with travel and food guides by writers from every continent; among the lavishly illustrated coffee-table books, there are titles on Rome featuring watercolours by Boschin's wife, the talented American artist Wendy Artin. Battered old leather suitcases and globes add to the atmosphere of the place. At the front, there is an extensive selection of vintage maps and prints, precious first-edition books by travel writers such as Pierre Loti, and rare finds like a manual of Neapolitan sign language. Life at the bookstore is so frantic that Bruno rarely manages to travel himself, but he can advise intrepid adventure seekers and armchair travellers alike on what to read however far away you want to go.

11 NuYorica

Piazza Pollarola 36–37

Stylish shoppers come for serious sprees at this sleekly designed shoe shop, whose white perspex display boxes are artfully arranged with vertiginously high heels, fringed leather bags and day-glow plastic sandals. It stocks every girl's favourite labels, from Marc Jacobs to Sigerson Morrison, and it also has a couple of rails of carefully chosen garments from labels such as Chloe, Pucci and the glorious Roman fashion brand Capucci, recently revived by the designer Maurizio Galante. NuYorica gets its name from Masters at Work's compilation record *Nuyorica*; there is always a funky beat as a shopping soundtrack, which, together with the comfy sofas, creates a club-like atmosphere. The service is relaxed and friendly rather than formal, and owner Cristiano Giovagnoli is on first-name terms with many of the customers.

FUN FOOTWEAR

12 Loco

Via dei Baullari 22

This small shoe store is for those who like their feet to have personality. Eschewing current trends in footwear, it sells a wide range of men's and women's shoes in unconventional shapes and stylish finishes: from 1950s bowling style to baroque jewel-encrusted stilettos, all the models are quirky and fun. Loco is the sort of place that attracts a regular clientele, who visit to satisfy a seasonal fix or to find something for special occasions. Owned by a TV costume designer and her sister, Loco argues the case against bland, branded shoes. Sunglasses by Bis & Curious and costume jewelry by Roman duo Iosselliani are among the accessories on display. The architects were Prater & Rossi, while many of the twirling hanging lamps were also designed by Iosselliani, who have deployed their trademark craftsmanship to create a shiny, sculptural space.

PERENNIAL FAVOURITE

13 La Vineria Reggio

156

Rosaria Mondello's eccentric taste, combined with the sheer delight in discovering new eyewear design talent, has made this store something of a cult; so much so that its followers have been dubbed '*mondelliani*'. You will recognize the spectacles in the street by their geometric, groovy shapes in dazzling colours. Rosaria believes that every face 'is a work of art' and so deserves a carefully conceived frame. She won't stock major Italian brands, but focuses on smaller names, such as the German Grotesque line, Parisian LaFont and the odd Cutler and Gross model. The shop's interior is as stylish as the frames. Undulating back-lit shelves are laden with sunglasses, and the accompanying flower installations are by nearby florist Il Giardino Segreto. There is a front window reserved for artists' installations: every month, artists such as Anna Romanello, Marco Petrella and Salvatore Pupillo unleash their imagination on a theme, using the shop's stock as inspiring props.

Sharing a space with Ilaria Miani's shop (p. 162), Iron Icon is a gallery-cum-shop showcasing the works of three Roman artist-designers, Stefano Antonelli, Alfredo Valente and Tommaso Ziffer. Of the three, Ziffer is perhaps the best known in architectural and design circles, having created the 1940s-inspired interiors of the Hotel de Russie with Olga Polizzi as well as the eclectic ambience of Casa Howard (p. 122). Stefano Antonelli's Art Déco–style bronze medusa lamps are arranged next door to Alfredo Valente's monumental sculptures cast in chalk, reminiscent of ancient Roman statues. The laid-back atmosphere is down to playwright and actor Roberto Agostini, who manages the gallery in his spare time, and will provide an informed commentary on the pieces for sale.

Pierluigi

FISH FANTASY
18 Hosteria del Pesce
Via di Monserrato 32

Recently opened and quickly established as the late dinner spot for the chic and wealthy clientele who live around the Campo de' Fiori, Hosteria del Pesce is a mecca for those who love Mediterranean fish. The owners, Johnny and Giuliano Micalusi, are former fishermen, and they buy all the fish and seafood at the nearby market of Terracina, where the daily catch is first class. At the entrance to the restaurant, lobsters, clams, langoustines and silvery sea bass are displayed on ice in a veritable culinary 'installation'. Just choose your fish and chef Franco will cook it for you. The starters are exceptional and include salt cod with potatoes, clam and langoustine carpaccio, and stewed octopus; for mains there are Catalan-style lobster, grilled red snapper and sea bass baked in a salt crust.

FIRM FAVOURITE
19 Pierluigi
Piazza dei Ricci 144

Pierluigi is the surname of the original family that owned this establishment between 1938 and 1980. The restaurant was a pleasantly old-fashioned Roman *hosteria* (a place where the host is often the cook) until Roberto Lisi and his wife, Pina, bought it and expanded into several more rooms and a large cellar. Pierluigi soon attracted a large following of locals, politicians and the odd celebrity. Regular clients confidently order their 'usuals', which might be a warm lobster salad, fragrant tagliatelle with courgette-flower sauce, or sliced seared beef with rocket. Pierluigi stands opposite Palazzo Ricci, a well-preserved 16th-century building, originally belonging to the Ricci family, whose façade is decorated with paintings. Palazzo Ricci is known for having been the home of the infamous Costanza Farnese, who is believed to have had an incestuous relationship with her father, Pope Paul III.

OPULENT STYLE
20 Fabio Salini
Via di Monserrato 18

A bank vault with protective walls and a secretive atmosphere is the inspiration behind Fabio Salini's atelier, created by the jewelry designer himself with some help from architect Massimo d'Alessandro. The interior has sumptuous Art Déco–style woodwork and furnishing, with silver leaf walls, white leather daybeds and cabinets encasing his precious necklaces and bracelets. Nothing is too opulent for this dandyish character, who trained at Cartier in Paris before coming home to Bulgari and then founding his own collection. His work is featured regularly in *Vogue Gioiello* and at Rome's haute couture fashion shows. Classic pieces to be found in his atelier include jade chokers encrusted with diamonds, earrings dripping with rubies, sapphires and emeralds, as well as bracelets in semi-precious stones. Queen Rania of Jordan is a fan of his delicate silverwork and lavish use of precious gems.

FUN AND FUNKY
21 Sisters
Via dei Banchi Vecchi 143

Sisters Eleonora, Emanuela and Veronica Nobile Mino – two are art historians and the youngest is an interior decorator – have made this store-cum-gallery an essential stop for anyone interested in contemporary Italian art and over-the-top decorative lamps, tables and mirrors. 'Our father is a collector and we grew up in his villa surrounded by busts, antiques and other eccentric finds,' explains the eldest sister, Eleonora. Quirky 1950s chairs found at flea markets around Italy incongruously sit next to lights by designer Angela Ardisson, while sculptural wrought-iron lamps and stuffed birds are mixed with large antique mirrors. Every couple of months, Sisters in Art promote a range of contemporary Italian artists, whose work is shown within the 'furnished' environment of the shop. Exhibitions of up-and-coming artists have included Giorgio Sabbatini, Daniela Perego and Michele de Andreis.

22 Il Goccetto
Via dei Banchi Vecchi 14

Sergio Ceccarelli caters to the thirsty crowd who work and play in the Campo de' Fiori area – shopkeepers, restaurateurs, bohemians. On balmy summer evenings customers spill out onto the narrow street, balancing a glass of wine and resting a foot on a parked Vespa. The cool and dark interior of this listed building, with its frescoed ceilings and rustic wooden chairs and tables, make it an informal retreat for an *aperitivo*. One of the precursors of the *enoteca* movement, which revolutionized the style of drinking in Rome, Sergio is always at hand to dispense knowledge to perplexed customers. He serves twenty wines, including champagne and prosecco, by the glass, and has hundreds of bottles stocked on the wood shelves, all carefully selected and with a particular emphasis on smaller producers. Italian and French cheeses, salads and meats from the famous Tuscan butcher Falorni are served swiftly from the marble counter.

A SUPERIOR BED & BREAKFAST
23 Relais Banchi Vecchi

124

DELICIOUS FARE
24 Boccon Divino
Vicolo del Pavone 2

Hidden between the back of the Hotel Relais Banchi Vecchi (p. 124) and the Palazzo Cesarini Sforza, il Boccon Divino restaurant is not to be confused with the establishment bearing the same name in Campo Marzio (p. 24). This is the nearest you will get in Rome to a restaurant offering a fixed-price menu – for around 25 euros diners are treated to a refined three-course meal and a jug of local wine – and its popularity among the young and fashionable crowd means that it often squeezes three sittings into one evening. Fish pie, veal meatballs in tomato sauce and pappardelle with wild boar appear among the selection of traditional dishes presented with a contemporary twist. The service can sometimes be shambolic, especially if cutlery is missing, and the décor is not exactly at the leading edge, but all that is forgiven in the cosy and friendly atmosphere.

SWIMWEAR SPOT
25 Laura Urbinati
Via dei Banchi Vecchi 50a

Laura Urbinati is the ultimate queen of the bikini. Step inside her small, white box of a shop and a riot of acid green, shocking pink and suave mauve models hanging from the rails will saturate your senses. Her swimwear designs have been collectable items for some years, so news that the Milan-based designer's second Italian shop would be in Rome was celebrated by her fans. Kaftans from Attik Battik, leather flip-flops and embroidered sheer dresses for a sundowner drink are among the essentials of every true Italian beach babe.

ITALIAN CLASSICS
26 Lo Scrittorio XXth Century Design
Via dei Coronari 102–3

Considering the recent proliferation of contemporary furniture shops stocking just about every European and American mid-modern classic, it is a delight to encounter XXth Century Design, a carefully assembled selection of period Italian pieces, ranging from the 1930s to the 1960s. Architect Raniero Aulenti has mixed true vintage finds with some of his own designs in a bid to offer 'a connection between the creative quality of early design and the manufacturing quality of the later industrial years'. Located on Via dei Coronari, traditionally the road with the most antiques shops in town, XXth Century Design stands out for being a mix between a design and an art shop. A recent visit revealed a 1926 head by sculptor Attilio Torresini (whose work is also on display in the city's Galleria Nazionale d'Arte Moderna), glass lamps by Venetian company Mazzega, and some 1969 reinforced fibreglass ribbon chairs by Franca Stagi and Cesare Leonardi for manufacturer Elco Bernini.

SMART SERVICE
27 L'Altro di Mastai

136

SISTER ACT
28 Il Bicchiere di Mastai

151

BOUTIQUE ROW

29 Via del Governo Vecchio

- SBU (Strategic Business Unit),
  Via di San Pantaleo 68–69
- Josephine de Huertas, no. 68
- Arsenale, no. 64

A street long associated with second-hand shops (see next entry) before 'vintage' became an overused term, Via del Governo Vecchio has over the past twenty years gradually become a long row of incredibly hip boutiques. Those seeking perfectly cut jeans should head for SBU, Patrizio and Cristiano Prefetti's popular shop, whose main claim to fame is the special denim woven in Japan and the USA but washed and sewn in the north Italian region of Veneto. Further up the road is Josephine de Huertas's boutique, a treasure trove of frilly dresses, sheer blouses and sexy stilettos. Next door is Arsenale, a quirkier place where the owner, Roman designer Patrizia Pieroni, sells her romantic flowing gowns, soft woolly coats and knitted scarfs.

VINTAGE FINDS

30 Vestiti Usati Cinzia

Via del Governo Vecchio 45

Cinzia has been selling second-hand clothes for most of her life, first from a tiny shop in Via del Pellegrino and, more recently, from the larger premises in Via del Governo Vecchio. She sources most of her garments from flea markets around Italy, and has an obvious talent for spotting rare, covetable pieces. The shop is a cavernous space where the more popular items, like military jackets, fur and leather coats and Pucci-style dresses, are stashed in the front. At the back is every stylist's dream, with cabinets laden with 1970s Chanel bags, 1960s Mary Quant sunglasses and 1980s faux zebra Dolce and Gabbana platform shoes.

FABULOUS FAKES

31 Tempi Moderni 1880–1980

Via del Governo Vecchio 108

This sweet costume-jewelry shop is run by Panama-born Elias Chaluja and his partner Pierluigi La Sala. For over thirty years, the two have been collecting mostly American costume jewelry by Trifari, Boucher and Pennino as well as indigenous finds, like Italian 1950s Murano glass-paste earrings. Items of furniture, such as Chinese screens, Art Déco lamps and French turn-of-the-20th-century paintings add to the mix.

More recently, Elias has been dressing his 1930s mannequins with bright, Futurist-style men's shirts.

DECONSTRUCTED DRESSES

32 L'una e L'altra

164

PLEASING PIZZERIA

33 Da Baffetto

Via del Governo Vecchio 114

Expect long queues at this historic pizzeria, where hearty meals are available at reasonable prices, although you cannot linger. Waiters whiz around the tables balancing six or seven plates at a time and the *pizzaioli* knead, flip and shove the pizzas in the large wood-fired oven. Baffetto's pizzas are legendary, their flat, crusty bases flavoured with toppings such as *marinara* (with anchovies), *funghi* (thinly sliced mushrooms), and *capricciosa* (artichokes, ham and eggs). This haunt is a perennial favourite of actors and celebrities, whose photographs hugging the moustached owner, Baffetto, adorn the walls.

COOL SPOT

34 Bar del Fico

155

BEAUTY PARADE

35 Bar della Pace

151

INTIMATE SURROUNDINGS

36 Enoteca Il Piccolo

Via del Governo Vecchio 74–75

Among the numerous bars that have sprung up along Via del Governo Vecchio recently, Enoteca Il Piccolo stands out for its lack of pretension, tiny proportions and excellent wine list. Housed in a 16th-century building, and furnished with a few rustic tables and chairs, Il Piccolo thrives on a faithful clientele who favour Giancarlo Davoli's selection of top Italian labels. Lunch is a modest menu of hams and sandwiches for local workers; for *aperitivo* try Mirtillino, a refreshing blueberry wine that arrives with a long spoon for scooping the berries out.

BEST OF BRAMANTE
37 Bramante Cloister
Vicolo del Arco della Pace 5

Donato Bramante's cloister, constructed between 1500 and 1504, attached to the theatrical Renaissance church of Santa Maria della Pace, was his first building in Rome. Divided into two storeys of arcades, Bramante planned the proportions of the arches to ensure remarkable effects of light and shade. Baroque and chamber-music concerts are held here in the summer as well as major art exhibitions.

BLOOMING BEAUTIES
38 Bloom

ESTABLISHED ENOTECA
39 Cul de Sac

LOFT LIVING
40 Magazzini Associati

SPLENDID SETTING
41 Piazza Navona

Piazza Navona is Roman 17th-century splendour at its finest. It was largely built for the Pamphilj Pope Innocent X (1644–55), who made it a memorial to his powerful reign. He first commissioned Rainaldi, then Borromini to design the extremely ornate church of Sant'Agnese in Agone next door to the Palazzo Pamphilj, and Bernini to create the central Fontana dei Quattro Fiumi. Continue to the north end of the square to peek at the ancient ruins from the small balcony just off Piazza di Tor Sanguigna, a reminder of how the square looked during Roman times, when it was used for aquatic games such as re-enacted water battles.

AMALFI AND ART
42 Santa Lucia
Largo Febo 13

For over twenty years Bartolo Cuomo held court at the nearby Bar della Pace (p. 151). Santa Lucia, a restaurant and bar located in the enchanting Largo Febo, is a more recent venture. It features a secluded terrace for outdoor dining, with cascading vines and wisteria. The décor recalls the 17th-century houses of his home town, Ravello, with hand-

painted tiles, and terracotta and ochre hues. On the walls are a few examples from Bartolo's contemporary art collection, donated by his friends the Italian artists Mario Schifano, Sandro Chia and Francesco Clemente. The menu is also dedicated to the flavours of the Amalfi coast: buffalo mozzarella, ripe tomatoes and oversized zesty lemons.

PRIVATE COLLECTION
43 Palazzo Altemps
Piazza Sant'Apollinare 44

Like many aristocratic family homes in Rome, Palazzo Altemps, built *c.* 1477, languished for centuries. Now part of the Museo Nazionale Romano, after extensive restoration work, it was opened in 1997 and features what is left of the original collection of Greek and Roman statues. The interior frescoes that remain have been restored, and some of the rooms are quite remarkable in their size and grandeur, in particular the chamber with a 15th-century fresco depicting the wedding presents given to Girolamo Riario and Caterina Sforza in 1477.

RENEWED CLASSIC
44 Hostaria dell'Orso

LOUCHE LOUNGE
45 Supperclub

HOUSE OF FUN
46 La Maison

SMALL BUT PERFECTLY FORMED
47 Il Simposio

OLD-FASHIONED REMEDIES
48 L'Antica Erboristeria
Via di Torre Argentina 15

Established in 1752, the Antica Erboristeria can claim to be the oldest herbalist in in Europe. The shop was certainly well-known in the 19th century, as it is mentioned in a famous sonnet by the Roman poet Gioacchino Belli. The quaint, original interior – Italian walnut cabinets full of dried herbs, and an old beamed ceiling – give the place a timeless atmosphere, although it has recently been extended to turn it into a more functional space.

Trastevere
Ghetto
Campidoglio

Via degli Orti d'Albert ④

Via delle Mantellate

Vic. di San Francesco di Sales
Via San Francesco di Sales
Via della Penitenza ⑤

Villa
Farnesina ①

Palazzo Corsini

Via Corsini

Parco
Gianicolense

Orto
Botanico ②

GIANICOLO

Via di Porta S. Pancrazio

Via G. Mameli

Largo di
Porta San
Pancrazio ③

Piazzale
Aurelio

Via Garibaldi

Via Giacinto Carini

Via Pietro Roselli

Viale delle Mura Aurelie

Villa
Sciarra

Via Dandolo

Viale Glorioso

Viale delle Mura Gianicolensi

Via Ugo Bassi

Via Alberto Mario

Via Nicola Fabrizi

Via Goffredo Mameli

Via A. Bertani

Via Luciano Manara

Via L. Santini

Piazza di
San Cosimato ⑫

Via Emilio Morosini

TRASTEVERE

Piazza
Trilussa

Piazza di
Santa Maria
in Trastevere

Piazza di
San Calisto ⑩

Via della Cisterna ⑪

Via della Lungaretta

Via della Paglia

Via della Pelliccia ⑦

⑥

⑧

⑨

Ponte Sisto

Lungotevere Farnesina

Lungotevere della Farnesina

Lungotevere dei Vallati

Lungotevere Raffaello Sanzio

Piazza Sidney
Sonnino

Via della Lungaretta

⑯

Via di Ponte Sisto

Piazza de
San Francesco
d'Assisi

Piazza
Mastai

Viale delle Mura Portuensi

Piazza
Bernardino
da Feltre ⑬

⑭
⑮

Viale di Trastevere

Viale Glorioso

Via Induno

Via Induno

Viale delle Mura Portuensi

Piazza di
Porta Portese

Lungotevere Ripa

Largo
Arenula

Via Florida   Via delle Botteghe Oscure

Via di San Marco

Piazza
Venezia

Piazza
Benedetto Cairoli

Piazza
Mattei ㉗

㉖

㉘

Via Arenula

Piazza de'
Cenci ㉕

㉔   ㉓

Piazza
Cinque
Scole

⑲

Piazza di
Campitelli

㉒

Piazza
Margana ㉙

Piazza
d'Aracoeli

Piazza di
Campidoglio ㉚

Palazzo dei
Conservatori ㉛

GHETTO

㉑   ⑳

Via Catalana

Teatro di
Marcello

Isola
Tiberina

⑰

CAMPIDOGLIO

⑱

Lungotevere dei Cenci

Lungotevere degli Anguillara

Piazza in
Piscinula

Piazza dei
Ponziani

Ponte Palatino

AVENTINO

Via Luigia San Felice

Via Marmorata

Via della Luce

Lungotevere Ripa

㉜

The other big historic heart of the city is Trastevere, so called because it lies across the other side of the Tiber. The neighbourhood includes the fabulous green spaces of the Orto Botanico (p. 66), Gianicolo hill and the Villa Pamphili. The art galleries and artists' lofts around the old prison of Le Mantellate attract a bohemian crowd, but slip over to Piazza Trilussa and its labyrinth of alleyways and its crumbling façades to get a sense of Rome of the past. Café culture thrives in the square in front of Santa Maria in Trastevere, with its glistening mosaics. Like many parts of Rome's historic centre, Trastevere is an edgy mix of well-heeled residents and authentic Roman characters. You will still find local boutiques, unpretentious bars and tiny workshops where artisans practise their craft as if caught in a time warp. The area around the market of San Cosimato is the centre of neighbourhood life, with stall vendors selling produce from the neighbouring countryside.

For those seeking pleasure, Trastevere is largely an evening stomping ground. And while the foreign resident population has inspired an unhealthy number of themed pubs and lacklustre trattorias, there are a few reputable establishments. Ferrara (p. 139) and Alberto Ciarla (p. 140) make the top grades in most food bibles, and a few established pizzerias never fail to disappoint. During the balmy summer evenings, the whole city decamps here for the Festa di Noantri, which unwinds itself through streets of stall vendors. *Noantri* means 'us', in contrast with *voiatri*, 'the other Romans', as if to reinforce the notion that Trastevere's inhabitants are the true Romans.

Head north across the Tiber to find the entrance to the old Jewish Ghetto, created in 1555 by Pope Paul IV, who imposed a curfew and forbade Jews from practising any trade other than rag or scrap iron. For the next three centuries Jews were confined to a tangle of insalubrious, dark roads and secret squares, bordered by the Via Arenula, the Theatre of Marcellus and the river bank. After the unification of Italy in 1870, the Roman Jewish community enjoyed a period of relative freedom, only to be crushed again by Mussolini's regime and the deportation in 1943 by the SS to concentration camps. Today the Ghetto has established a villagey charm, where spacious apartments have captured the attention of diplomats and academics, turning it into one of the city's most prestigious addresses. Yet the original community's spirit still lives on: elderly residents pull up a chair on the street for a leisurely chat, while kosher restaurants along the Via del Portico d'Ottavia ply the gastronomic treats of Jewish Roman cuisine. For culture, head eastwards to Campidoglio, or Capital Hill (p. 77), to discover a wealth of museums and archaeological sites that celebrate the origins and history of the Eternal City.

RENAISSANCE VILLA

1 Villa Farnesina
Via della Lungara 230

Walking down the busy Via della Lungara you reach an
ivy-covered gate that leads into the tree-lined grounds
of Villa Farnesina, once the home of 16th-century banker
and art patron Agostino Chigi. Designed by Baldassare
Peruzzi between 1506 and 1510, the villa is renowned for
its exquisite frescoes created by Raphael and Peruzzi. In
the Loggia of Cupid and Psyche, the ceiling decoration
is a pergola of fruit and flowers. Raphael's stunning
Triumph of Galatea, in the loggia of the same name,
features a nymph driving a scallop shell chariot pulled
by frisky dolphins. Popular legend claims that Chigi
allowed Raphael's mistress, La Fornarina, to live here
while he worked so that the painting would be completed
more speedily. Today the villa is the seat of the Accademia
dei Lincei, one of Italy's most distinguished centres
of learning; it also houses the Department of Drawings
and Prints.

GREEN OASIS

2 Orto Botanico
Largo Cristina di Svezia 24

It is fitting that these lush botanical gardens should be in
Trastevere, traditionally one of the greenest areas of town
– the nearby streets bear names like Orti (gardens) della
Farnesina and Via delle Fratte di Trastevere. At the foot of
the Gianicolo hill, the well-kept botanical gardens are
filled with tropical palm trees and greenhouses containing
all kinds of prickly cactus species, while uphill a
beautifully scented rose garden is filled with ornamental
species fashionable in the Baroque era. Children are
attracted by the garden's central fountain; lovers lose
themselves in the zigzagging paths of the shady bamboo
forest; and serious botanical enthusiasts, accompanied by
a detailed guide, spot the rare medicinal plants that
flourish here. Because entrance is by ticket only, the
gardens retain their charm as a secluded and secret spot
lying right in the centre of the bustling but sometimes
over-touristed part of Trastevere.

SMOOTH OPERATOR

3 Antico Arco
136

R · XIII

TRASTEVERE

PASTICCERIA

Valzani

Specialità
DOLCIARIE ROMANE

PONTE
SISTO

As much a patron as an art dealer, Lorcan O'Neill recently left his London outpost – he was formerly with the Anthony D'Offay gallery – to set up this contemporary art gallery in Trastevere. The voluminous space occupies the ground floor of a converted stables just next door to The Film Studio, one of the city's oldest repertory cinemas and a favourite hang-out with the film-making scene during the 1960s. O'Neill believes that it is a good time for art in Rome. 'In the last couple of years Italian art has been receiving a great deal of attention,' he says, especially with the commissioning of the new MAXXI and Macro art venues (p. 41). As well as Italian painters like Luigi Ontani, the gallery has brought international artists to the city: Kiki Smith, Jeff Wall and Tracey Emin have been among the gallery's highlights, initiated into the Roman art world with a rowdy party or two.

One of the first galleries of international contemporary art in Rome – Massimo Mininni and Norberto Ruggeri opened it in 1994 – Sales is now competing with new kids on the block Lorcan O'Neill and Roma Roma Roma, all situated in the arty quarter of Trastevere. However, Sales, situated at the foot of the Gianicolo hill, is still the venue to check out rising American, British and Italian artists. Jane and Louise Wilson and Wolfgang Tillmans's shows have recently graced the walls, and the gallery also shows art of the past with recent displays of work by Alighiero Boetti and Yves Klein.

Now in her eighties, Virginia Valzani has been running this shop specializing in Roman patisserie since she was fourteen, and she shows no signs of slowing down. Although these days it is her son who bakes and decorates the cakes in the *laboratorio* at the back, Virginia holds court at front of house, cheerfully retelling anecdotes about ancient and contemporary eating habits. She claims that two of her Roman specialities, *torrone romano* (a variation on the Italian Christmas sweet traditionally made of dried nougat) and *maritozzo* (a bread-like dough filled with whipped cream) have a phallic shape because they were originally baked to celebrate ancient Roman weddings. Many of her pastries include ingredients such as honey and dried fruit, described by Pliny the Elder in the 1st century AD. Some of today's favourites are the *diavoletti*, chocolate pralines spiced with chilli, dark chocolate sachertorte and the famous Nana cake, which is a whipped cream-topped chocolate *semifreddo* originally conceived for the 1960 Rome Olympics.

It is hard to find a street in Trastevere that is not now packed with touristy restaurants, English-style pubs and dull boutiques, so small, good establishments certainly deserve attention. Named after the seven deadly sins, Vizi Capitali is aimed at the young international crowd as well as Trastevere's more discerning diners. The décor is understated and a little rustic, the highlight being seven paintings depicting variations on those deadly sins. The theme continues on the menu, with dishes named after characters from Dante's *Inferno*, but they are reassuringly more divine than comic. Owners Catalina Croitoru and Marco Scandola are followers of the Slow Food movement, which is reflected in their inventive menu with a good selection of regional dishes, which might include melon carpaccio with bacon, ricotta cheese with rocket salad, spaghetti with langoustine, courgette flowers with a lime sauce. The successful wine list was devised by chef Giovanni Lucchetti to find the perfect enhancement to the flavours of his fine cooking.

TEA AND BOOKS

11 Bibli
Via dei Fienaroli 28

With its high ceilings, packed bookshelves and spacious reading rooms, Bibli is an unexpected find at the end of a small Trastevere side street. The store has more than 30,000 books to browse among, including a fair number of foreign language offerings, and serves as a multicultural venue for literature, live music, films and talks. Bibli has also attracted the thriving Roman web-surfing community, who take delight in the comfy chairs and plentiful computers and find it a welcoming space in which to spend a few hours. Writers and film directors come here to present their latest efforts to an always attentive audience. Sunday brunches at the restaurant are a popular choice, so is tea served in the cosy café on the terrace.

ECCENTRIC AMBIENCE

12 Alberto Ciarla
140

BARGAIN HUNTER PARADISE

13 Porta Portese
Porta Portese, Viale di Trastevere

For those visually saturated by the glitzy boutiques of the city centre, and in search of true one-offs, a visit to Porta Portese can bring unexpected pleasure. Arrive early at this popular flea market or you will risk finding little left to buy. Every Sunday morning, from 6 a.m. until 2 p.m., crowds flock to pick up bargains along the route, which starts from the gate of Porta Portese and winds along Viale Trastevere. The market still has a vague air of illegality, a legacy from its origins as a black market during the Second World War. The so-called 'Russian area' is where most of the bric à brac is located, in between the racks of old fur coats, leather bags and battered suitcases. Off Piazza Ippolito Nievo are the more 'respectable' stalls selling Indian furniture, Italian country-style antiques, old laces and linens, costume jewelry, plants, bicycles and even pets. Further down one can find stalls selling inexpensive, new clothing. Rummaging has been elevated to a rather high art in Porta Portese, so a slow rather than frantic approach to bargain-hunting or haggling should bring extensive rewards.

SPINNING DECKS

14 Suite at Ripa Hotel
Via degli Orti di Trastevere 1

The Suite club at Ripa Hotel has a life of its own. Like the hotel, it was designed by Anglo–Italian architectural practice King & Roselli and features the progressive contemporary style for which they are known. As the sun goes down, it sheds its calm and collected atmosphere when 'Professor' Pierandrea, one of the capital's most popular DJs and the club's artistic director takes control of the space. Wednesday is dedicated to R'n'B lovers, Thursday is gay disco night, and Saturday brings the pumping sounds of house and electro. Pierandrea brings in other Roman DJs, Flavia Lazzarini and Nino Scarico, to name a couple, as well as those from the international circuit, so a fun night out in a groovy ambience is guaranteed throughout the week.

ÜBER-MODERN STYLE

15 Ripa Hotel
126

SHOW TIME

16 Roma Roma Roma
Via dell'Arco dei Tolomei 2

Serious contemporary art collecting has been given a shot of new life with the opening of Roma Roma Roma, the brainchild of Gavin Brown, a New York gallery owner, Toby Webster, director of the Modern Institute of Glasgow, and Franco Noero, a Turin art dealer. Their collaboration has created a gallery space that, with its modern interiors, stands out in the tiny medieval arched road of Via dell'Arco dei Tolomei. That such a powerful team of international dealers should open a gallery here is further proof of how Rome is developing as a vibrant centre for contemporary art attracting international talent. Recent group shows, which have featured the work of photographer Robert Mappelthorpe and Martin Creed and Italian artists Francesco Vezzoli and Bruna Esposito, and individual shows are present in the airy rooms and the gardens.

RESTAURANT WITH A VIEW

17 Sora Lella
143

18 La Sinagoga
Lungotevere dei Cenci

Crossing over the antiquated bridge that connects Isola Tiberina with the entrance to the old Jewish Ghetto, you catch a first glimpse of the towering synagogue. The elaborate marble structure was completed in 1904 as a symbol of Jewish liberation after three centuries of oppression. Inside, the sanctuary features columns from Assyria, gilded friezes and a copper-hued cupola. There are remnants of arks saved from synagogues destroyed during the Ghetto period. Upstairs a small museum displays tapestries, eternal lights and a 15th-century Torah. Set amidst all this splendour, as a reminder of Roman Jews' long and often sad history, a plaque commemorates the one killed and forty wounded by a terrorist attack in 1982. Another plaque recalls the rounding up of 2000 Jews in 1943, from which only fifteen returned. After the war, survivors of the Holocaust could still be encountered as they went about their daily business in the Ghetto, their concentration camp numbers indelibly tattooed on their arms.

KOSHER FOOD
19 La Taverna del Ghetto
Via del Portico d'Ottavia 8

Located right at the heart of the Ghetto, this family-run Jewish restaurant is located in a 14th-century palace; a fountain at the entrance remains for the ritual washing of hands. Inside, the restaurant is designed as a medieval tavern, with exposed brickwork and the odd Roman column. The menu is kosher and features many of the specialities of Roman Jewish cuisine: layered anchovies and curly endive salad, deep-fried vegetables, *bottarga* (dried cod roe) with cherry tomatoes and beef stew Jewish style, plus ricotta and cherry cake for dessert. For liquid refreshment, mint tea and kosher wines are available.

DINING UNDER THE ARCH
20 Giggetto
Via del Portico d'Ottavia 21a–22

Although its owners are Catholic, Giggetto is known for its crunchy *carciofi alla giudia* – a Jewish dish where whole artichokes are flattened into the shape of a chrysanthemum and then deep fried. Other delicacies on the menu include spelt soup, fried calamari, battered salt cod and pasta carbonara. The owner, Luigi Ceccarelli,

a.k.a. Giggetto, founded this *hostaria* in the 1920s when his dislike for Fascist politics made him switch from a career as a train master to one in catering. His son Franco and nephew Claudio continue to run this white-linen tablecloth restaurant with the same sense of hospitality, maintaining its reputation as a dining place for special occasions for local families and professionals. The outdoor setting is unique: tables are placed under the Portico d'Ottavia, which Augustus dedicated to his sister in 23 BC.

AUSTRIA MEETS AMERICA
21 La Dolce Roma
Via del Portico d'Ottavia 20b

Wedged between the kosher restaurants that line the Portico d'Ottavia strip, La Dolce Roma first appears an unlikely proposition. Even though owner Stefano Ceccarelli comes from a tradition of Jewish Roman cuisine (his father runs Giggetto next door), he has opted for an American- and Austrian-inspired patisserie. Dolce Roma is no more than a counter and a few chairs, but the crumbly blueberry muffins, apple pie, wildberry yoghurt cheesecake, and his heavenly dark chocolate sachertorte are enough to keep customers coming back for more. Stefano also bakes rustic breads with sunflower, rye or wholemeal flour.

PLEASURE SPOT
22 Ristorante Vecchia Roma
Piazza di Campitelli 12

Vecchia Roma is everything you can ask of a restaurant in Rome: it is located in the attractive Piazza Campitelli, on the borders of the old Jewish Ghetto; it has the stunning Santa Maria Campitelli next door; and it serves superb food. Dining alfresco is very much the point here as no interior could compete with the beauty of the surroundings. The four rooms try their best, with oil paintings and gilded mirrors – the back room is apparently favoured by movie stars in search of privacy. There has been a restaurant on these premises since 1911, but true fame among hedonistic diners came when Antonio and Giuseppe Palladini took it over in 1973. Try the seafood starter, the gnocchi with cherry tomatoes and pecorino cheese or the fillet of turbot with a broccoli sauce. For dessert there are *granite*, cold meringue soufflé, and flaky pastry with ricotta cheese and dustings of bitter cocoa.

23 Sora Margherita
Piazza Cinque Scole 30

Only those in the know will find Sora Margherita as it has no outdoor labelling. Since 1927 this quaint little restaurant has been serving food and a glass of Velletri wine to the working-class inhabitants of the city. Today its paper-clad tables and wicker chairs are graced by locals, students and the odd government minister. After Sora Margherita (which in Romanesco dialect means Mrs) retired, new management took over, and the restaurant is now also open on Friday and Saturday evenings. However, very little has changed. Every morning at 6 a.m., a hundred fresh eggs are delivered and Signora Gianna arrives to make fresh fettuccine, agnolotti, gnocchi and maltagliati pasta. Cook Lucia, who used to work with Margherita, runs the kitchen, serving Roman classics like chick pea and pasta soup, salt cod in *guazzetto* (a sauce made with tomatoes, pine nuts and raisins) and slow-cooked tripe. More innovative culinary treats include rigatoni with ricotta (instead of the traditional pecorino), and ground pepper and kosher veal sausages with polenta.

24 Bleve
Via di Santa Maria del Pianto 9a–11

This used to be Anacleto Bleve's original wine bar and store before he moved to more palatial premises (p. 152). Now turned into a smaller wine shop, the wine labels on offer still prove his enthusiasm for the art of drinking. Top Italian producers from Piedmont and Tuscany (try the Sassicaia Cabernet if you can afford it), as well as rising Lazio labels Castel de Paolis and Casale del Giglio, sit alongside high-class offerings from Australia, South Africa, California and Chile. Liquors and digestifs hold pride of place – cognac, armagnac and grappa – as do aged balsamic vinegars from Modena. A selection of delicacies in jars, such as Sicilian tuna in olive oil with sun-dried tomatoes, stuffed red peppers, red onion chutney and black truffle paste, means anyone can take away a memento of Italian gourmet style without breaking the bank.

25 Ristorante il Pompiere
Via di Santa Maria dei Calderari 38

Lovers of tranquil surroundings come to Il Pompiere to enjoy simple Roman food and courteous service. Run by the Monteferri family since 1962 and named after a fireman ancestor, it is one of the old Ghetto's most evocative palaces, once the home of courtesan Beatrice Cenci. Frescoed rooms, dark wood panelling and views over the pretty Piazza Cinque Scole (the restaurant is on the top floor) provide a perfect background for work lunches or family outings. One of the restaurant's notable strengths is the soup menu. Try pasta and broccoli on Monday, pasta and beans on Tuesday, spelt soup on Wednesday, gnocchi on Thursday and pasta and chick peas on Friday, all served with crunchy bread from the nearby town of Lariano. The Catholic owners and cooks will also rustle up Jewish Roman specialities, such as the crunchy, deep-fried artichoke *carciofi alla giudia* or battered fried cod.

26 San Daniele
Piazza Mattei 16

The original bar San Daniele is in the Friuli town bearing the same name, and Rome is where this chain of refined wine bars started its expansion. Owned by a consortium of San Daniele producers and farmers, they aim to spread the word about their mouth-watering sweet hams, zesty wines and aromatic grappas. All the wines on the list are produced by the Fantinel family, since 1969 the producers of labels like Sant'Helena, Santa Caterina and Borgo Tesis. Try them with a cold salad of ham, figs and pineapple or warm *crostini* (toasted bread) with ham and cheese. Housed in the Palazzo Mattei, the bar's interior has the atmosphere of an illicit drinking den, decorated with 19th-century cabinets, country-style tables and chairs and a gleaming red 1950s ham slicing machine. The medieval door at the back adds to the air of mystery: it is the original one from which persecuted Jews escaped during the Second World War to hide in the cavernous, secret passageways of the Ghetto.

27 Bar Tartaruga
Piazza Mattei

Those with idiosyncratic tastes will be satisfied by the eccentric ambience of Bar Tartaruga. With its plush sofas, bordello red walls, faux-crystal chandeliers, plastic flowers and draped curtains, it transports nocturnal visitors to somewhere near Marrakech c. 1974. On second thought, it could almost be the set of a Fellini film gone Technicolor, but then things always get misty at a certain hour. Bar Tartaruga is a magnet for late-night drinkers who sip their cocktails while singers entertain with jazz songs or a Roman-style cabaret. A row of outdoor seats in the square allows you to contemplate life while gazing at the wonderful turtle shell decorated fountain in Piazza Mattei.

VIBRANT VIBE

28 Le Bain
Via delle Botteghe Oscure 33

Owned by the same nightlife impresarios who run La Maison (p. 159), Le Bain is a lounge-bar-cum-club-cum-restaurant that attracts a largely young crowd at night, but also a mix of wealthy professionals and style-conscious travellers at lunchtime and in the afternoon. Housed in the former stables of a 16th-century palace, the interiors are a mélange of shabby-chic drink cabinets, colourful lights by Jacopo Foggini, and art by Mark Kostabi and Rome-based Malaysian artist H. H. Lim. Come here around 7 p.m. to sip an *aperitivo* at the candlelit long bar, or to dine at the restaurant where chef Vito Rossano serves traditional Roman dishes. Freshly baked bread and cakes are also on offer and the cellar boasts over 650 wines. Later in the evening there is a live bossa nova set by Brazilian maestro Legalia; the upstairs bar becomes a small dancing area where fashionable DJs take to the decks.

OASIS OF CIVILITY

29 La Taverna degli Amici
Piazza Margana 36–37

As you leave the old Ghetto, and before you climb the numerous stairs that lead to the Campidoglio hill, take a break at Piazza Margana, a charming square filled with vine-clad palaces. On the corner stands La Taverna degli Amici, a simple restaurant hidden by the lush foliage and signposted by a marble plaque. On sunny days, a

leisurely meal at one of the outside tables, away from the roaring traffic of nearby Piazza Venezia, is a secluded experience. True Roman food is how the owner Mauro Volpi describes his menu, and the selection includes gutsy *amatriciana* pasta (with tomato and pancetta), *spaghetti cacio e pepe* (with Pecorino Romano and crushed peppercorns), succulent steaks and delicate roasted milk-fed lamb. A delicious ginger sorbet makes a satisfying end to the meal.

CAPUT MUNDI

30 Campidoglio

The best way to approach the Campidoglio, or Capitoline hill, is by climbing the long flight of stairs that leads from Piazza d'Aracoeli to the top. Once at the summit, you are rewarded by the sheer beauty of this grand, dramatic square, conceived by Michelangelo. Right in the very centre stands the statue of Marcus Aurelius (a copy), riding on his horse and silhouetted against the golden-hued Palazzo Senatorio, the seat of the city's government. The pavement is decorated in an intriguing interplay of ellipses and volutes that Michelangelo designed. On both sides of the square, flanked by the statues of Castor and Pollux, are the Musei Capitolini, housed in the twin palaces Palazzo Nuovo and Palazzo dei Conservatori, which contain Greek and Roman sculptures and paintings by Rubens, Caravaggio and Titian; in the courtyard are the remains of the iconic colossal statue of Constantine II from the 4th century.

DRINKS ON THE TERRACE

31 Caffeteria Capitolina
Piazza Caffarelli 4

It is a short stroll from the Capitoline Museum to the Caffeteria Capitolina roof terrace, signposted by an entrance at the back of a 16th-century palazzo. The service is slow and the food over-priced, but the unique view is worth resisting the outrage for. Sip your prosecco or freshly squeezed orange juice while admiring the gleaming rooftop of the synagogue and the ancient ruins of the Theatre of Marcellus.

ROMANTIC DINING

32 San Teodoro

137

Aventino
Testaccio
Ostiense

CAMPIDOGLIO

Vico Jugario
Piazza della
Consolazione

PALATINO

Tempio di
Fortuna Virile
Ponte Palatino
Piazza della
Bocca della
Verità
Tempio
di Vesta

Via di San Teodoro

TRASTEVERE

AVENTINO

Parco di
Sant'Alessio

Circo
Massimo

Parco
Savello   **2** Via di Santa Sabina
                              Roseto
3 Piazza   Piazzale
        Pietro   Ugo
        d'Illiria   la Malfa
                    1

Piazza
di Porta
Capena

Piazza
Sant'Alessio   Piazza
4   Giunone Regina
Piazza dei
Cavalieri   Piazza del
di Malta **5**   Tempio
                   di Diana
                          Piazza di
                          Santa
Piazza   Prisca
Sant'Anselmo

Ⓜ
CIRCO
MASSIMO

Roseto
Communale
di Roma

Piazza
Albina

Piazza
del Servili

Piazza
Albania

6

Via Giovanni Branca
Piazza di
Santa Maria
Liberatrice
Piazza
Testaccio **10**
           9 **8** **7**
                         Largo
                         Manlio
                         Gelsomini
Viale Manlio Gelsomini
                         Parco della
                         Resistenza
                         dell' 8 Sett.

11 Via Galvani

16   TESTACCIO

Piazza Orazio
Giustiniani   **14**
18   Monte
                   Testaccio
15   **12**
13   **17**

Piazza
di Porta
San Paolo

Piazzale
Ostiense

Ⓜ
PIRAMIDE

Ponte Testaccio

Piazza
Vittorio
Bottego

V. di Campo Boario
Via Giovanni da Empoli

OSTIENSE

Via del Porto Fluviale

21
Via dei Magazzini Generali

20
Via del Commercio

Piazza del
Gazometro

Approximate scale

1/2 kilometre

1/4 mile

19

The whiff of new money fills the air on this ancient hill of Rome. Aventino is a classy neighbourhood that looks down on the Palatine from its palatial gardens and pricey villas. Swimming pools, a rare commodity in Rome's historic centre, add to the burgeoning prestige. The quiet tree-lined streets, punctuated by empty squares, feel pleasantly residential, with only a few determined tourists to be found following the trail of churches. Aspiration levels gradually drop down into busy Via Marmorata, which marks the entrance to traditional, working-class Testaccio. Rome's former meatpacking district, Testaccio's name derives from the Latin word *testum*, meaning terracotta fragment. During Roman times, Testaccio was a river port where olive oil, wine and grain would arrive from the provinces in huge terracotta urns, which were then emptied and thrown into a heap. Over the years, the debris formed *Il monte dei cocci* (the mount of fragments) or Monte Testaccio. Grottoes that were dug in the hill for cellars are now the location for nightclubs that attract a more hedonistic type of cave dweller.

Testaccio combines remnants of traditional Roman life with an edgier, thriving night scene. By day, the fruit and vegetable market is the epicentre of local life, where streets are peppered with modest trattorias serving the cuisine of Quinto quarto (the fifth quarter). At night, the noise levels rise and it is transformed into a pleasure seeker's route of clubs, cafés and outdoor gig venues. Testaccio manages to cling to its proletarian roots, despite the influx of writers, artists and young students. Its working-class culture was defined when it became the setting for the municipal slaughterhouse in 1890. Although closed in 1973, its influence on the area remains and it is now being converted into a cultural centre. A grid of social housing projects for the slaughterhouse workers is the residential backbone of the area, which retains the typical features of large courtyards and small apartments for crowded living. Paradoxically, many original slaughterhouse workers still live in Testaccio, making it one of the areas with the highest concentration of elderly people in Rome.

Past the Pyramid of Caius Cestius starts Ostiense, identified by trendspotters as the 'new Testaccio'. While Ostiense lacks the village charm of its neighbour, its industrial architecture has made it fertile ground for nightlife impresarios and enlightened restaurateurs who have converted its warehouses and disused power stations into drinking dens, clubs and starkly designed eateries. The population is still largely night owl, but the city's soaring property prices might well push the design crew to this side of town soon.

1 Il Roseto Comunale di Roma
Clivio dei Pubblici

The rose garden on the climb towards the Aventine hill offers welcome respite just off the grand, grassy space of the Circo Massimo where horse and chariot racing used to take place during ancient Roman times. Established in the 17th century as the site of a Jewish cemetery, in 1950 the area was transformed into communal gardens. To commemorate the connection with the Roman Jewish community, the avenues were landscaped in the shape of the menorah. The garden's peak time is May, when hundreds of rose species blossom luxuriously creating a pastel-coloured maze of plants. Like many sections of the wealthy Aventino area, the gardens feel a million miles away from the hustle and bustle of daily life. Nannies with prams, dog walkers and couples in search of fleeting intimacy come here to wallow in the delicious wafts of rose perfume.

PARK WITH A VIEW
2 Parco Savello
Piazza Pietro d'Illiria

There are two ways to reach these intimate belvedere gardens: the steep walled path of the Clivo di Rocca Savella or the Santa Sabina main road that passes next to the rose garden. Whichever route, be prepared to enjoy one of the most breathtaking views of the city, with the Tiberina island just below, St Peter's looming in the distance and all of the city's rich antiquity laid out before you. Parco Savello is also known as *Il Giardino degli Aranci* because of its delightful orange trees, planted in memory of St Dominic, who is said to have introduced Spanish orange trees to Italy in 1220, and legend claims that the original tree survives in the nearby gardens of the church of Santa Sabina. The garden occupies the walled area of the old Savelli fortress and is believed to be the site of Emperor's Otto III's palace.

ROMANESQUE IN ROME

3 Santa Sabina
Piazza Pietro d'Illiria

With such an abundance of churches in Rome, it is easy to become nonchalant about the city's sacred architecture. Santa Sabina stands apart for being the most perfectly preserved example of an early Christian basilica of the 5th century that reveals its connections to Roman building traditions. It was founded in 425 by Pietro D'Illiria on the site of a villa owned by a Roman matron called Sabina. It was the first Dominican church, dedicated by Onorio III to St Dominic in 1222. Outside the façade is stark in its simplicity, inside twenty-four matching Corinthian columns create a magnificent space, illuminated by the golden sunlight that pours in from the windows. The main carved wooden doors are beautifully maintained and feature scenes from the Old and New Testaments. Next door is the Dominican monastery: on request, visitors may visit St Dominic's cell and the 13th-century cloister.

KEYHOLE VISTA

4 Priorato dei Cavalieri di Malta
Piazza dei Cavalieri di Malta 4

Designed by the visionary architect-artist Piranesi, the Piazza dei Cavalieri di Malta is a cleverly engineered square punctuated by small obelisks, trophies of arms and tall cypresses. Crowds gather here to peek through the keyhole in the door to the Knights of Malta to admire the perfectly framed vista of the dome of St Peter's, flanked by an avenue of trees. But this outlook is not just a pretty picture. it is a view that encompasses three countries – the Italian State, the Priory, which is the residence of the Great Master of the Order, and the Vatican, a sovereign state. Not to be overlooked are two gems that face the square, Santa Maria del Priorato, also designed by Piranesi and considered by some to be the least-known masterpiece of 18th-century Rome, and the International Benedictine church of Sant'Anselmo, from which, on Sunday evenings, you can hear the celestial sound of Gregorian chants during vespers.

5 Il Negozio Benedettino della Badia Primaziale di Sant'Anselmo

Piazza dei Cavalieri di Malta 5

This quaint shop, located inside a hut that flanks the Sant'Anselmo Abbey, sells goods produced in monasteries from all over the world. Specialities are the abbey's own chocolate – prettily packaged in old-fashioned paper wrappers – beers made by Trappist monks, and soaps from the Monastery of Subiaco. Dispense with the liturgical prayer books and focus on the excellent cosmetic section, offering miraculous creams against cellulite and wrinkles, and the extracts of blueberries or devil's claw, which promise relief from all sorts of ailments. Organic fruit juices, jams and tomato sauce will guarantee heavenly meals.

6 Augustarello

Via Giovanni Branca 98

By day, Testaccio sheds its clubby, underground image and returns to its proletarian roots with the food market and several restaurants serving the community. Via Branca was the setting for one of the first AS Roma supporters' clubs, and faded yellow and red murals still adorn the road's walls in testament to its *tifosi* (fans) heritage. Augustarello, like all good neighbourhood haunts, attracts its share of lunch and dinner regulars who bask in the cosy, unassuming service. Two unadorned rooms and a small summer garden is all it is. The menu is reassuringly Roman: lamb and potatoes, artichokes with mint, and typical gutsy Testaccio dishes like *rigatoni alla pajata*, which is made from milk-fed veal's intestines.

On the front price tag: *formaggio* **PECORINO DI FOSSA** *40.80* INFOSSATURA 2003

MORE FOOD

7 Volpetti

Via Alessandro Volta 8

It makes perfect sense that the Volpetti deli should expand into a *tavola calda*, a lunchtime, paper-tablecloth food joint where lucky customers can sample their fabulous ingredients. The bakery and the kitchen at the back ensure a constant supply of warm pizza and fragrant pies stuffed with chard, ricotta and spinach, olives and capers. On the front counter there is selection of ready-made dishes, such as lasagne, octopus salad and meatballs. The interiors are functional rather than stylish, but the place is always teeming with loyal customers and local workers.

GOURMET DELI

8 Volpetti

Via Marmorata 47

Customers complain that they can never leave Volpetti without buying much more than they bargained for; certainly the staff here excel at persuading you to buy delicacies from all over Italy. Owners Claudio and Emilio Volpetti have run the place since 1973, gradually transforming it from a local *alimentari* into a gourmet pilgrimage site. The shop prides itself on specializing in several types of hams, such as Prosciutto di Norcia, Parma and San Daniele e di Montagna as well as Parmesan, buffalo mozzarella and goats' cheese. Their Pecorino Romano comes from sheep that graze the neighbouring countryside, and speciality breads are delivered daily (sample their fragrant bread from Altamura in the Puglia region on Tuesday and Friday).

HOME-STYLE COOKING
9 Da Felice
Via Mastro Giorgio 29

Felice Trivelloni is a *burbero* (meaning gruff), classic Roman character who won't mince his words if he doesn't like you or you don't eat up your food. But if you don't rub him up the wrong way you will fall victim to his good heart and culinary talents – the eighty-four-year-old still shops every day at the Testaccio market and insists on preparing dishes like *carciofi alla romana* (stewed artichokes with mint) himself. Felice attracts legions of fans – most notably Oscar-winning actor Roberto Benigni who even composed a poem in his honour, now framed on the wall. Expect unfussy, traditional fare – on Friday it's salt cod, Saturday is tripe, and Tuesday is pasta with lentils and beans.

BUSTLING LIFE
10 Mercato di Testaccio
Piazza Testaccio

The epicentre of Testaccio life, this noisy, odoriferous covered fruit and vegetable market is the real thing. It is not particularly pretty – stalls are functionally rather than decoratively stacked with piles of artichokes from nearby Ladispoli or tomatoes from Pachino, Sicily – but the produce is as fresh as it is cheap. Valentino's stand is celebrated in its own right every Tuesday and Friday when elderly women from the countryside drop off bags of hand-picked *misticanza* salad – a mix of wild chicory, small wild onions, fragrant mint leaves, dandelions and spicy rocket.

BAR STRIP
11 Via Galvani
- Joia Music Restaurant, nos 20–22
- Ketumbar, no. 24
- Bush, no. 44
- Letico, no. 64

Over the past ten years, Testaccio has evolved from meatpacking district into a hedonistic hotspot with rows of clubs, bars and restaurants all clustered around the old slaughterhouse area. Nothing much starts here until after 11 p.m., when young crowds and cars descend on Via Galvani turning it into a traffic-jammed road. Watering holes include Joia, a minimally furnished three-floor bar-restaurant-club whose 17th-century-inspired lounge provides a decadent setting for nocturnal

cocktails. On Wednesdays DJ Luca Agnelli spins the decks in the all white disco. Next door stands chic Ketumbar, one of the first bars in town to attempt an indigenous version of Paris's Buddha bar, combining Indo China–inspired minimalism with vernacular features such as pieces of Roman amphorae. The fusion sushi-nasi goreng-style cuisine comes in small portions and high prices, but it is still a good place for a post-dinner drink. House and techno are played at Bush, a two-storey disco bar decorated with black-and-white snaps of celebrities, while Letico is another of the area's standbys, a restaurant and bar decked out in warm dark wood and clean lines.

CLUB ROUTE
12 Via di Monte Testaccio
- Café de Oriente, no. 36
- Akab, no. 69
- Caffè Latino, no. 96

Round the corner from Via Galvani, just in front of the old slaughterhouse, is another maze of cavernous clubs and bars, dug out from the old cellars that used to line the *Monte dei Cocci*. Despite the oriental mood, squashy cushions, incense and Buddha statues, Café de Oriente's musical forte is Latino, with Cuban bands and dance acts. Further on is Akab, which combines electro-dance nights with a 1970s-inspired flea market every Sunday at 6 p.m. Further along, Caffè Latino is the historic 'disco pub' of the area, a place to catch live concerts and a good selection of funky acid jazz, house and reggae tunes. An ethnic vibe is imposed with Indian textiles and cushions, while low lighting makes it the perfect drinking den.

COMMUNITY SPIRIT
13 Villaggio Globale
Via del Monte dei Cocci 22

A constant source of entertainment, Villaggio Globale is one of Rome's oldest *centro sociale* – self-regulating community centres with a penchant for art and live music, usually located in old disused warehouses and factories. While the current restoration of parts of the municipal slaughterhouse is taking place, Villaggio Globale has partly decamped to the large tent that has been erected within its walls. In the summer, Villaggio Globale organizes music and even the odd gay festival, with live reggae concerts, stalls selling artefacts, kiosks with *panini* and beers, and a general happy vibe.

FIFTH QUARTER CUISINE
14 Checchino dal 1887

137

GAY SCENE
15 Alibi
Via di Monte Testaccio 40–44

The original gay club in town, Alibi democratically caters to a mixed crowd. Its three floors are dug into the side of *Monte dei Cocci* – at the top a panoramic terrace provides a vantage point for checking out Testaccio's continuous procession of night tribes. The club has a large dance floor, two bars and a private area reserved for VIPs. Expect themed music – deep house, dance and latin with a gay slant. Drag shows are not unknown, the most popular being *Sanremo* night, with imitations of Italy's celebrated song festival.

UNDERGROUND THEATRE
16 Teatro di Documenti
Via Nicola Zabaglia 42

Created from a 15th-century building, the Teatro di Documenti has abolished conventional notions of divisions between actors and the audience. Instead of staying in your seat, you are transported on a journey that follows the story as it unravels to a subterranean level and then returns back up. All sorts of shows take place here, but the best performances are those that make the most of this atmospheric setting – Monteverdi's *Orfeo e Euridice*, a tale of descent into hell, is particularly poignant. The theatre also hosts exhibitions and can be visited by prior appointment.

CELEBRITY TOMBS
17 Cimitero Inglese
Via Caio Cestio 6

On the edge of the Testaccio area rises the distinctly un-Roman Pyramid of Caius Cestius, built in the 1st century BC after the defeat of Cleopatra. Behind it lies the English Cemetery, created in 1700 for the burial of non-Catholics. Enter it via the gate (if shut ring for the keeper) and walk through the tall cypresses and well-tended flowers. The cemetery attempts to recreate the simplicity of an English country churchyard and is a haven of secluded calm. Visitors pop in to see Keats's tomb, where Trelawney buried Shelley's heart and Goethe's son's grave.

CULTURAL CENTRE
18 Macro al Mattatoio
Piazza Orazio Giustiniani 4

The Testaccio branch of the Museo d'Arte Contemporanea (p. 41), has taken over two newly restored pavilions in the slaughterhouse area. Together with Villaggio Globale, the Architecture Faculty of Rome's University and the School of Popular Music, this area is set to become a vast 'City of the Arts'. Meanwhile, exhibitions of contemporary Italian artists are on show until late at night.

CHARMING COLLECTION
19 Centrale Montemartini
Via Ostiense 106

Inaugurated in 1921, the Centrale was the first electric power plant in Rome and is a highlight of early-20th-century industrial architecture. Now it is the home of the superb collection of Hellenic statues from the Capitoline Museums: marble sculptures stand among boilers, hydraulic pumps and steel tubes in a fascinating combination of the ancient and relatively new.

NIGHT TRIBES
20 Alpheus
Via del Commercio 36

Alpheus is arguably Testaccio's most established venue and still thrives on its happening reputation. A warehouse conversion, the club has three halls, each hosting differently themed musical zones. Live concerts, cabaret shows and even tango lessons are some of the club's offerings, although its forte is the bacchanalian dancing that takes place on weekends with house DJs Lusky and Jimmy J. A wild night out.

WAREHOUSE OF FUN
21 Ex Magazzini
Via dei Magazzini Generali 8 bis

Another favourite hang-out of the bold and beautiful nightclubbing set, Ex Magazzini is housed in a converted warehouse and offers entertainment at all hours. You can start with an *aperitivo or* perhaps see some theatre or a film. Later on, reggae, house or drum 'n bass themed nights kick off. On Sundays, the club's lower ground floor becomes the site for a large ethnic market, selling wares from India and Indonesia to appropriately inspired eastern tracks.

San Lorenzo
Esquilino
Monti

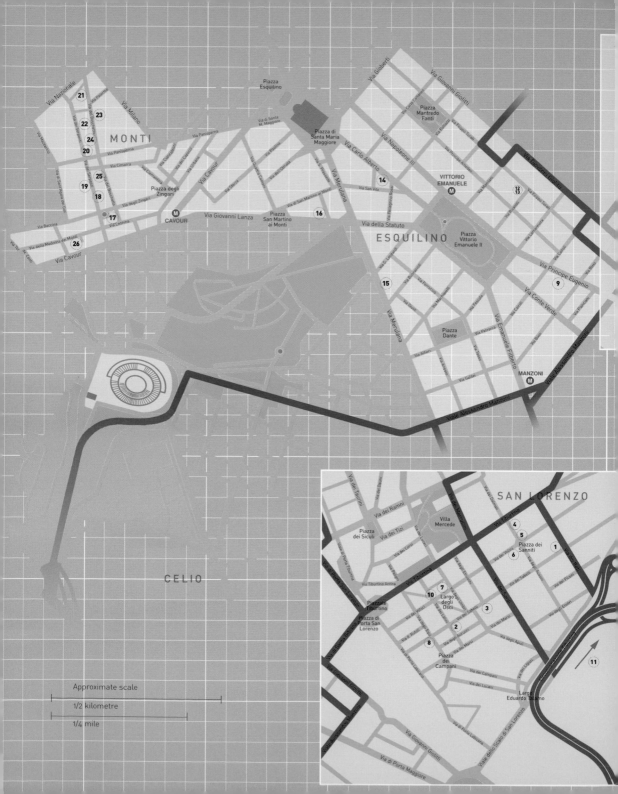

MONTI

Via Nazionale
Via Milano
Via Panisperna
Via Cavour
Via Panisperna
Via Urbana
Piazza degli Zingari
Via degli Zingari
Via Baccina
Via della Madonna dei Monti
Via Leonina
Via Cavour

21
23
22
24
20
25
19
18
17
26

Piazza Esquilino

Piazza di Santa Maria Maggiore

Via di Santa M. Maggiore
Via Paolina
Via Carlo Alberto
Via Napoleone III
Via Merulana
Via San Vito
Via Giovanni Lanza
Piazza San Martino ai Monti
Via di San Martino ai Monti

14
16

Via Gioberti
Via Giovanni Giolitti
Piazza Manfredo Fanti

VITTORIO EMANUELE
Ⓜ

CAVOUR
Ⓜ

ESQUILINO

Via della Statuto
Piazza Vittorio Emanuele II
Piazza Dante
Via Emanuele Filiberto
Via Merulana

15

Via Principe Eugenio
Via Conte Verde

9

12
13

MANZONI
Ⓜ

Viale Alessandro Manzoni

CELIO

Approximate scale

1/2 kilometre

1/4 mile

SAN LORENZO

Via dei Ramni
Villa Mercede
Piazza dei Siculi
Via dei Tizi
Via dei Sabelli
Piazza dei Sanniti

4
5
6
1

7
10
Largo degli Osci
3

Piazzale Tiburtino
Piazza di Porta San Lorenzo

2
8

Piazza dei Campani
Via dei Campani
Via dei Luceri

Largo Eduardo Talamo

11

Via Giovanni Giolitti
Viale dello Scalo di San Lorenzo
Via di Porta Maggiore

Monti has the been the last of the city centre's historic areas to resist gentrification, but is now reputed to be one of Rome's more happening addresses. It still retains a down-to-earth atmosphere, with its creeper-clad streets and few piazzas in which everyone seems to know everyone else. Its past reputation as a poor and seedy district dates back many centuries: the Emperor Claudius's promiscuous wife Messalina would famously search for pleasure in Monti's alleyways and brothels. Now the quarter is crowded with antiques shops, chic thrift boutiques and buzzing wine bars.

Head south-east for the Esquilino, Rome's highest hill. The streets around Piazza Vittorio Emanuele II and the Termini station form a multiethnic centre in a city otherwise indifferent to outside cultural experience. Coexistence between the resident Roman middle classes and the recent immigrant community is so far serene, and the area has benefited from an injection of multiculturalism. Set among the 1870s Umbertini-style buildings are Chinese emporiums selling Suzy Wong-style dresses, flanked by Ethiopian pharmacies. The stalls of the new covered food market are saturated with aromas of ginger, coriander, plantain and yam; and here, too, can be found the unusual sight of halal butchers. Not far away are restaurants like Agata e Romeo (p. 145) and bakery Panella (p. 99), putting their own particular spin on traditional Roman food. Closer to Termini station are several Ethiopian and Eritrean restaurants. Recent landmarks such as Radisson SAS hotel (p. 130) have been adopted by residents who enjoy its stylish Zest bar (p. 99). Meanwhile, the lacklustre Modernist Termini station, started in 1936 by Angiolo Mazzonis and finished in 1950, has been recently renovate, and transformed into a modern mini retail centre.

East of Termini lies the San Lorenzo quarter, the only part of Rome to be seriously bombed during the Second World War. It is ironic that this area, which was home to so many of Mussolini's political opponents, should have suffered the most devastation by Allied forces. Today the empty shells of the homes that were destroyed stand as a poignant reminder. The nearby university provides San Lorenzo with a large student population, which has no doubt encouraged the transformation of this neighbourhood into a vibrant, all-night venue for bars, cheap trattorias and clubs. The bohemian population has its headquarters in the converted lofts of the old pasta factory Cerere, where designers and artists work, live and play. The core appeal of San Lorenzo is that it remains authentically working class, with Roma's supporters' clubs, anarchist books stores, a bustling food market and many traditional restaurants cohabiting with fashionable new eateries.

STREETCAR STYLE
1   Tram Tram
Via dei Reti 44–46

VEGGIE DELIGHTS
2   Arancia Blu
Via dei Latini 55, 65

Named after the tramline that runs along the Via dei Reti, Tram Tram was one of the first restaurants to open in San Lorenzo in the 1980s serving 'innovative' traditional Italian food. Family run, Tram Tram has a south Italian tinged menu for the first courses, while the seconds are inspired by Roman cuisine. Hearty starters include broad bean mash with chicory; mains are *Pugliese orecchiette* with broccoli and clams, swordfish rolls and anchovies, and endive salad terrine. The décor cleverly employs disused train parts that have been converted into wine racks and banquette seating in the bar area. The railway reference dates back to the early 19th century, when San Lorenzo was where the railway workers' housing associations were built.

Since 1993, Fabio Bassan has been serving vegetarian fare to the trendy inhabitants of San Lorenzo, probably converting a couple of meat-eaters on the way too. His mantra is that you can be a vegetarian restaurant without being a 'punitive' one. The innovative menu reflects this belief; for example, a salad of artichokes is served on a bed of creamed chick peas, followed by *maccheroncini* with truffles. For those who still have the appetite there is zabaione with a crunchy toasted pine-nut topping. The homey décor makes it a good place for lunch; try it before a visit to Galleria Pino Casagrande.

CANDLELIGHT DINING

3 Il Dito e la Luna
Via dei Sabelli 51

Sicilian Cosimo Grassadonia devised this superior bistro as a place to sample good wines (there is an excellent list of over 350 labels) and well-executed food at reasonable prices. Serving only in the evenings, this is an elegant, candle-lit restaurant; the dining room upstairs is favoured by the romantically inclined. The menu includes a range of subtly flavoured south Italian classics, from a red onion flan to a salad of fennel, black olives and oranges, and pasta with anchovies and breadcrumbs. Celebrated Sicilian sweets such as ricotta-filled pastry rolls compete with a truly mouth-watering chocolate soufflé.

ART AT HOME

4 Galleria Pino Casagrande
Via degli Ausoni 7a

Fitting well with an area that has become the favourite location for the new *Scuola Romana* of contemporary art, Pino Casagrande decided to open the doors of his Art Déco–style townhouse to art hungry visitors. Over the years, the textile magnate has amassed a collection of antiquities and contemporary art. American minimalism is well represented by Donald Judd, Sol Le Witt and Dan Flavin, while his constantly changing selection also includes pieces by British artist Julian Opie. Furniture by Ettore Sottsass, Alvar Alto, Mies van der Rohe and Le Corbusier is scattered within a domestic setting and the beautiful, geometric garden contributes to an aesthetically pleasing moment.

This famous establishment has been serving its range of gutsy Roman cuisine since the 1970s to intellectuals including film director Pier Paolo Pasolini, who loved the down-to-earth, populist soul of the San Lorenzo area. Today, Pommidoro is patronized by the artistic community who live in the nearby 'Pastificio Cerere' (an old pasta factory and mill converted into studio spaces) as well as by stars of the Roma football team. The service is friendly and low key – waiters address regulars by their first names and owner Aldo will often come out from the kitchen to share anecdotes about local history. Grilled meats are a speciality, as is the *spaghetti alla carbonara* and *alla gricia* (with bacon and a good dose of ground pepper). For regular customers a treat is the traditional Roman delicacy, *rigatoni all pajata*, which is made with veal's intestines and has been effectively outlawed since the BSE scare. It is a creamy and delicate dish. The best seats are in the outdoor annex looking on to the square – often the site of impromptu concerts.

Milan-born designer Myriam Bottazzi has been crafting expressionist pieces of jewelry for the past twenty years, building a clutch of faithful followers, including fashion designers Martine Sitbon and Romeo Gigli, for whom she has created a number of accessories. The embodiment of a San Lorenzo resident, Myriam B's tiny showroom is a stone's throw away from her apartment, allowing no distractions from her constant stream of creativity. Chunky bronze brooches, hairclips with flower decorations, necklaces with arabesque motifs: nothing here is overstated, but they are the ideal bijoux for those who know how to make an entrance.

The San Lorenzo neighbourhood may have been gentrified over the years, but it has never forgotten its working-class roots. Artisan and wine shops, fresh food and vegetable markets still form the heart and soul of this quarter, so it is reassuring to see local traditions live on in designers like Claudio Sano and Myriam Bottazzi. Sano is an enthusiastic designer-maker who combines exquisite craftsmanship with a talent for creating highly individualistic forms and almost surrealist shapes. From his hand-stitched sandals to his handbags for women, briefcases and belts for men, everything reveals Claudio's love for leather, which he expertly treats, smooths and cuts. Great attention is given to the smooth finishes, the stitching and dyeing. His quirky briefcases with the keyhole cut out of them are instantly recognizable. This is a true find in the sea of globally branded leather accessories for which Italy has become so well known.

No Sunday afternoon *passeggiata* would be complete without a visit to Fassi, the ice-cream parlour favoured by true *gelato* connoisseurs. It has been around since the beginning of the 20th century, and the spacious parlour, furnished with tables and chairs, is a fine example of populist Art Déco style. On warm summer evenings, Roman families congregate here to taste the *ninetto*, a chocolate and cream flavour, or the Sicilian *cassata*, packed with candied fruit. Their *semifreddo* selection is also first rate – try the one with berries. Takeaway desserts are bound to impress the most sophisticated hosts, especially if you just happen to mention where they came from. The 'palazzo' has another shop in the Prati area, but the Via Principe Eugenio branch is the original.

WINE CORNER

10 Ferrazza

Via dei Volsci 59

Perched on the corner of Via dei Volsci facing the market square, the Ferrazza *enoteca* is conveniently placed for a bit of San Lorenzo people spotting. Local artisans and artists make this their favourite spot for an *aperitivo* – a common ritual now in Rome, imported from the north of Italy, which involves a drink or two before dinner with a delectable array of snacks. For the price of a glass of prosecco you can savour a vast selection of warm morsels of pizza, olives, crisps and miniature sandwiches. Orlando Ferrazza takes great pride in his cellar, which has over a thousand Italian wine labels plus a good selection by the glass. Oysters and raw fish dishes are among the choices on the light menu served in the narrow dining section. The interior is minimally stylish, with the attention focused on the bottles on display. Ferrazza is always packed, so arrive early.

MUSICAL CHAIRS

11 La Palma

158

TRAINSPOTTER'S DELIGHT

12 Radisson SAS

130

CAPPUCCINO AT THE TOP

13 Bar Zest

Via Filippo Turati 171

If you are not going to splash out on one of the Radisson SAS's ultra-modern suites, then you might as well take the lift to the seventh floor and enjoy the more democratic prices of Zest, its stylish bar and café with gritty views over the city. On days when the sun is out, Piazza Vittorio locals, the film and art crowds, all come here to read their Sunday papers with a cappuccino and *cornetto*, enjoying the decked patio and its views over the Termini railway station and the new covered market. Inside, Jasper Morrison chairs by Cappellini line up along the black granite bar to create the perfect cocktail ambience.

FAMILY AFFAIR

14 Agata e Romeo

145

THE ART OF BREAD

15 Panella

Via Merulana 54–55

Panella has people crossing town for just one bite of their fragrant warm breads. Bakers since 1920, the Panella family have researched their subject in depth, and sell around eighty varieties of bread. Some of the breads have been re-created from those discovered in Pompeii and written about by Pliny the Elder in the 1st century AD. Bread with herbs (rosemary, rocket and sage), crunchy Sardinian wafer-thin bread, Jewish Azzimo bread without yeast, crusty Roman *casareccio* and baguettes are just some of the items to choose from. Pizza, with tomato, courgette or cheese toppings, is always warm, and there is a fair selection of appetizers, such as deep-fried mozzarella, rice croquettes and savoury pies. At Easter out come an enormous variety of *pizze pasqualine*, filled with cheese and ham; while Christmas calls for imaginative variations on the *panettone* theme – one might be chocolate covered and another stuffed with custard cream. The store's new café offers cappuccinos and freshly squeezed fruit juices, as well as a delicious selection of Neapolitan pastries, croissants and Danish pastries.

SIMPLE FARE

16 Monti Doc

Via Giovanni Lanza 93

This cosy and always crowded *enoteca* sits anonymously on the trafficky Via Giovanni Lanza, just before it opens up to the splendid Piazza San Martino ai Monti with its medieval tower. It marks the entrance to Monti, an area packed with wine bars and *enoteche*. Inside, there are wooden tables, pots of dried flowers and an old-fashioned marble counter. Spelt soup with pumpkin, a *parmigiana* of aubergines and polenta with boar stew may be among the hearty dishes that change daily according to season and are listed on the board. The well-priced, regional wine list is one of the *enoteca's* selling points, and there is also an extensive selection by the glass. It is worth booking in advance.

DARK STARS
17 La Bottega del Cioccolato
Via Leonina 82

That La Bottega del Cioccolato closes for three months from June until September is proof of this chocolate shop's total commitment to freshness. Maurizio Proietti has chocolate running through his veins as his father was one of the original founders of the equally delicious chocolate shop Moriondo e Gariglio (p. 17), and, like his father, the Piedmontese tradition of chocolate making is the secret behind the mouth-watering selection made in the *laboratorio* at the back. The beautiful deep-red décor provides an ideal background to the dark, Brazilian 90 per cent cocoa bars. There are fruit jellies, nutty *torrone* sticks for Christmas, truffles, pepper- or cinnamon-infused bars, chilli chocolates and even miniature chocolate Colosseums. Pretty boxes of confectionery, coloured ribbons and personalized packaging add a refined touch.

AUSTRALIA MEETS THE MED
18 F.I.S.H – Fine International Seafood House
Via dei Serpenti 16

When they moved back to Rome after a childhood in Australia, Matteo and Paolo Bassi missed the Pan Asian-tinged food of Sydney so much that they decided to open a sushi and sashimi restaurant that would remind them of home. Of course, this being the Mediterranean, it was impossible not to take note of the plentiful local fish available; hence, while the Japanese inspiration is never far away, the menu also has an Italian spin. From the clam soup with ginger to the turbot carpaccio, the taste is top rate. The interiors – steel chairs, lacquer-style tables and low ceilings – are very modern, and there are plans to open up the snug space a bit. Their cellar of 120 labels is pioneering, with a good selection of Tasmanian, Australian and Kingsland producers, as well as Italian and French. And if you are just feeling peckish, don't miss out on the oyster bar at the front, a must among the cognoscenti of the area.

SIMPLE PLEASURES
19 Al Vino Al Vino
Via dei Serpenti 19

So many locals pop in here for a drink after work that it is easy to think of Al Vino Al Vino as the living room of the Monti area. The place has a relaxed and friendly vibe. The space is arranged around three rooms, with scaffolding and a counter salvaged from a 19th-century grocery store. The back room often works as a gallery space for art and photo exhibitions, while the small garden is a sweet little corner of respite. The food here is principally Tuscan inspired, although Giacomo's mother cooks a mean Sicilian *caponata* of aubergines. A wide wine list is available by the glass and there are lots of different grappas.

DESIGNING INTERIORS
20 Atelier Monti
Via Panisperna 42

After a spell in New York, architect Massimo Lucarini decided to join forces with Roberta De Angelis and open Atelier Monti, a contemporary interior and product design store. Their pride and joy are the beautifully crafted kitchens in solid oak, produced in the Veneto region by manufacturer Oldline, but smaller items include Venini glass and Pepe Cortes and Covo accessories. The interior of Atelier Monti is airy and well designed, a welcome injection of contemporary style in an area full of traditional antiques stores.

AUTHENTIC FLAVOURS
21 Valentino
Via del Boschetto 37

Originally a beer parlour, according to the recently restored 1930s sign, the Valentino restaurant stands out as a real find among the constantly growing crowd of trendy wine bars and eateries in Monti that in food terms do not always live up to their promise. Valentino is what Rome does best: a family-run trattoria complete with attentive, personal service. The speciality of the house is *scamorza*, a smoky provolone-like cheese, originally from southern Italy, served grilled with an infinite variety of toppings. Try it with rocket, mushrooms or Parma ham. Also excellent are the grilled meats, including a very good, juicy hamburger. For dessert, taste the fabulous *gelato* from nearby ice cream parlour Fassi (p. 96). Water it all down with wine from Lazio – the Casale del Giglio chardonnay is top rate.

FRANÇOIS
BOUTIQUE

PFAFF

22 François Boutique
Via del Boschetto 3

Model, DJ, fashion designer and now shop owner, Francesco Estela is a young man with many talents. His menswear store is inspired by 'the French boutique of the 1970s', although he admits that his clothes are directed to the 'metrosexual' customer. T-shirts with punk motifs, flamboyant shirts and vinyl day-glow belts hang on rails decorated with plastic flowers, all set against a huge Hawaiian landscape. His DJ decks and sewing machine are always on view. This shop is always a good place to stop by to pick up leaflets on the trendiest night club events in Rome, either organized by Francesco himself or by his group of funky friends.

PAST AND PRESENT
23 Le Gallinelle
Via del Boschetto 76

Over the years, Le Gallinelle has successfully graduated from a second-hand shop into a fully-fledged own label, albeit still keeping the retro spirit alive with its quirky choice of materials and shapes. Wilma Silvestri's Greek goddess-inspired draped evening dresses, pretty paisley patterned sundresses and fancy floral skirts are just some of the designs on display. A small selection of vintage Gucci bags, Valentino belts and Ben Sherman shirts for men, make it a destination for bargain hunters and discerning fashion stylists. The store's name is both a play on the more common name for the star constellation Pleiades as well as a reference to its previous incarnation as a butcher's shop. The original marble counter with chickens engraved on it, the hooks from which the meat was hung and the patterned tiled floor have all been kept in their original condition, blending seamlessly with the multicoloured garments hanging from the rails.

LEADING LIGHTS
24 Maria Teresa Gaudenzi
Via del Boschetto 1b

Maria Teresa Gaudenzi is a doyenne of 19th- and 20th-century finds. Clients from all over the world ask her to source rare and collectable items, and her pieces are often found in antiques shops around Europe. A specialist in Italian lights, especially Murano ones from the 1950s, 1960s and 1970s, she will also make bespoke designs. Her shop is a treasure trove of different eras from different countries; a 1940s Italian red bar cabinet sits alongside turn-of-the-20th-century Russian paintings, while a French Rococo-style glass dressing table contrasts with a bleached Swedish chest of drawers from 1800. This shop is an inexhaustible source of wonders.

A SENSE OF DRAMA
25 Fabio Piccioni
Via del Boschetto 148

Fabio Piccioni's small and cluttered shop is a shrine to glittering costume jewelry – from the better-known American makes like Trifari to rarer items such as Italian 1930s brooches and snake-shaped bracelets. Fabio rents out much of his collection for TV and theatre productions as well as using his training as a costume designer to create bespoke commissioned pieces. Hanging on the walls of the shop are signed photographs from grateful Italian actresses. Fabio himself is something of an eccentric character, often seen wearing necklaces and bracelets from his stock in an effortless way. Everywhere beads and buttons are stacked in boxes waiting to be used for the next production.

FLOWER POWER
26 Pastore & Tjäder
Via della Madonna dei Monti 62a

The regeneration of Monti has brought with it a new breed of hip inhabitants who want their terraces landscaped in a contemporary style. Eleonora Pastore and her Swedish partner Susanne Tjäder have tapped into the zeitgeist with their charming flower shop carved out of a medieval townhouse at the foot of the Monti area. In particular Susanne has imported into Rome a northern European sensibility towards horticulture and design, which has added something new and fresh to local florists. When not selling heady scented roses or pale pink peonies to passersby, they work as garden consultants or stylists decorating events like weddings, receptions and parties. The shop also stocks some seriously stylish vases, pots, containers and scented candles.

Colosseo
Celio

ESQUILINO

Viale Cesare Ceradini

Largo della
Polveriera

Viale del Monte Oppio

Via degli Orti di Mecenate

V. del Monte Oppio

Parco
di Traiano

Via delle Terme di Tito

Via Merulana

Largo
Gaetana Agnesi

Viale Serapide

M
COLOSSEO

Via Nicola Salvi

Viale della Domus Aurea

1

Viale di San Telemaca

Piazza
del
Colosseo

Colosseo

Viale di San Telemaca

Via Labicana

Arco di
Costantino

Via San Giovanni in Laterano

Via Merulana

Via Labicana

5

3

Via dei Santi Quattro Coronati

2

Via Celio Vibenna

7

12

Via Ostilia

6

9

Via Capo d'Africa

PALATINO

Parco
del Celio

Via del Parco del Celio

Tempio di
Claudio

8

4

Via Marco Aurelio

Via dei Querceti

Via di San Giovanni in Laterano

Via Annia

Via dei Santi Quattro Coronati

Via di San Stefano Rotondo

Via Claudia

Via Celimontana

Via San Gregorio

Piazza dei
Santi Giovanni
e Paolo

CELIO

Piazza
San Giovanni
in Laterano

Clivo di Scauro

Piazza Celimontana

Via di San Paolo della Croce

Via di Santo Stefano Rotondo

Piazza
di
Porta Capena

Via della Navicella

Via di Villa Fonseca

Santo Stefano
Rotondo

11

Villa
Celimontana

Via delle Mura Latine

M
CIRCO
MASSIMO

10

Via di San Sebastianello

Via di Santo Stefano Rotondo

Via di G.S. Erasmo

Via delle Mura Latine

Piazza
di Porta
Metronia

Via di Porta di Capena

Piazzale
Metronia

Via di Porta San Sebastiano

Piazzale
Numa
Pompilio

Via di Porta Latina

Approximate scale

1/4 kilometre

1/8 mile

Dubbed the 'Caelius Village' by its cheerfully partisan residents, the streets around Il Celio are undergoing a renaissance, especially since the opening of the Hotel Capo d'Africa (p. 132) in 2002. Bars open until late, neighbourhood trattorias and upmarket establishments serve innovative fare, small boutiques and art galleries run by the local artistic community provide an atmosphere of conviviality. In the summer, the serene gardens of Villa Celimontana (p. 113) become the site of a well-respected jazz festival. Keith Jarrett has played here but you also get good quality home-grown talent like jazzman Roberto Gatto. By day, Il Celio is a well-trodden sightseeing path, with some of the most stunning churches in the city. Before the unification of Italy in 1870, and the construction of an architectural grid that attempted to reorder the city, Rome was pretty much a landscape of parks, gardens, ancient ruins and a smattering of randomly located churches. The Celio manages to retain this flavour of old Rome, thanks to the creation of an archaeological park in the 19th century, which extends to the stone-paved Appia Antica. Walk round the Celio and discover its rambling warren of uphill and downhill streets, crumbling palazzi and secret architectural jewels. During ancient Rome's Imperial years this was where aristocratic families had their villas; Nero capriciously built his luxurious palace Domus Aurea (p. 108) on the hilly area of the Colle Oppio. Today the park is a pleasant green oasis, with walkers, cyclists and children enjoying its grassy slopes.

The archaeological epicentre of the area is without doubt the monumental Colosseum, now incongruously set in the middle of the major traffic artery of the Fori Imperiali. The Flavian Amphitheatre, as it was known in ancient times, is a remarkable feat of architecture and engineering. Its huge circumference is 545 metres, and it was conceived to host an unruly crowd of about 50,000 people. Started by the Emperor Vespasian in AD 70, it was inaugurated by his son Titus in AD 80 and finally completed during Domitian's reign (AD 81–96). Next to it stands the Arch of Constantine, a landmark erected in 315 by the Senate and the people of Rome to commemorate the Emperor's victory over Maxentium in 312.

The battles and games held inside the Colosseum meant that the headquarters of the gladiators were located in the Celio, along with the barracks for the Emperor's cavalry and provincial troupes. Many African Roman citizens used to live in the area, following a path of life similar to that narrated in Ridley Scott's film *Gladiator*. The streets were, therefore, an early cosmopolitan mix, a legacy that today's more affluent residents are keen to stress as they see their neighbourhood head towards 21st-century globalization.

1 Domus Aurea
Viale della Domus Aurea

Nero's Golden House has only recently been restored to its surprisingly sombre beauty after having been filled with rubble for many centuries. Built as a palace for the hedonistic pursuits of this unpopular Roman emperor, it is said to have covered an area twenty-five times the size of the Colosseum and to have had its own parkland and lake. Devastated by fire in AD 104, the site was then obliterated by his successors who drained the lake and built the Colosseum. When some of its buried rooms were discovered in the 15th century, no one realized that this was the fabled folly. However, the stunning paintings and decorations soon attracted the interest of antiquarians and artists who rushed to study them. Lowered by a rope, they would admire the frescoes by candlelight and often leave graffiti on the walls as a testament to their visit. Both Raphael's and Giovanni da Udine's decorations for the Vatican *Loggie* are said to have been executed in 'grotesque' style (natural forms that change into human or half-animal, half-human shapes) after the paintings of the Domus Aurea. Not to be missed, the Domus Aurea can be visited by prior telephone booking.

THREE CHURCHES IN ONE
2 Basilica di San Clemente
Via di San Giovanni in Laterano

At a quick glance this seems a typical example of 12th century architecture, but step inside and you will be treated to a fine example of multilayered history. The Basilica of San Clemente is the site of three successive places of Christian worship, built one on top of the other between the 1st and the 12th centuries. While the top church contains the Chapel of St Catherine of Alexandria, with frescoes by Masolino and, perhaps, by Masaccio, as you descend into the dark depths of the 4th-century lower basilica you are greeted by a fresco of the Empress Theodora Christianized into a Madonna. Here is also a fresco in comic strip style that features one of the earliest examples of the Italian language. Further down the steps you encounter a well-preserved Mithraeum, the focus of an ancient and curious Roman cult devoted to Mithras. The running water of an ancient stream nine metres below, used by the resident Irish Dominicans during the Second World War, reminds you of Rome's mysterious subterranean life.

LOCAL TALENT
3 Galleria Arte e Pensieri
Via Ostilia 3a

Just off the Via San Giovanni in Laterano is the recently opened art gallery Arte e Pensieri, which is run by the cultural association I Diagonali, an art collective comprising local artist Marisa Facchinetti and Testaccio residents Bruno Aller and Aldo Bertolini. The gallery features four exhibitions a year, but it also acts as an alternative meeting point for artists who are not part of the more established circuit. Unlike areas such as San Lorenzo, which already have an established artistic community, Galleria Arte e Pensieri is a pioneering project, putting the Celio neighbourhood on Rome's art-production map. Exhibitions have included Italian artists Giulio Turcato, Emilio Vedova and Achille Perilli. The interiors are unspectacular, but it is a good place to spot up-and-coming talents and has an interesting, rough, authentic feel about it. The opening times are slightly erratic so it is worth checking in advance when exhibitions are on.

CHARMING CHURCH
4 Santi Quattro Coronati
Via dei Santi Quattro Coronati

Walking uphill on the narrow Via dei Santi Quattro Coronati, visitors will catch a glimpse of the brickwork of what looks like a medieval castle. The church of Santi Quattro Coronati is the only fortified abbey in Rome, and was used in medieval times as a temporary papal residence or as a lodging for important guests. It is named after the four soldiers, Claudius, Nicostratus, Symphorian and Castrius, who were martyred under the Emperor Diocletian for refusing to worship the god Esculapius. The church's most charming asset, however, is the small cloister, accessible by ringing a bell and making a small donation. Inside, you are transported back to a peaceful world centuries old, as the central fountain tinkles away and the sun light filters through the arcades.

MORE THAN JUST COFFEE
5 Café Café

Via dei Santi Quattro Coronati 44

This intimate café, with buttery yellow walls and dark wood rustic-style chairs and tables, does more than just serve coffees. It is the selection of sixty different teas that steals the show here, as well as the very good wine list which focuses on 'medium bodied' varieties. Hearty chick-pea soup, large tasty salads, Greek and Spanish cheeses and homemade pastries are among the food offerings. Open from breakfast until two o'clock in the morning, it is a cheerful addition to the area's growing café culture and a good place to stop during a church sightseeing tour.

LUNCH STOPOVER
6 Papagiò

Via Capo d'Africa 26

Opened on the ashes of Magna Roma, a truly bizarre establishment famed for serving an 'interpretation' of ancient Roman dishes, Papagiò's real forte is in feeding the locals its blend of traditional dishes, fresh seasonal produce and smart service. Fresh fish is the speciality of the house, so good renditions of *spaghetti alle vongole* and *risotto agli scampi* are served, but the courgette flower and clam pasta is also excellent. The fine wine list emphasizes whites. After your meal, enjoy an afternoon *passeggiata* under the shady palms of Villa Celimontana.

Its name reflects the restaurant's specialization in crustaceans – largely crabs, langoustines and lobsters imported daily from Sardinia that swim in the large fish tank at the entrance, unaware of their future. But there are also raw fish carpaccios, stewed squid with potatoes and a warm Catalan salad on the menu. Previously an old warehouse, Crab has been transformed into an airy, chic space by architect Terry Vaina, with only some vibrantly coloured art on the walls to add a dramatic flourish. Sardinian father and daughter Eligio and Valentina Damu run this linen tablecloth establishment with effortless charm, and it has quickly risen as the new venue for the Eternal City's smart set and the nearby residents of Hotel Capo d'Africa.

GRILLED MEATS
9 Le Naumachie
Via Celimontana 7

A stalwart of the Celio area, Le Naumachie is the place to satisfy your carnivorous instincts. Fillet steak and roast beef are served with a traditional *contorno* (side dish) of potatoes and vegetables, and don't miss the house speciality, *fettuccine Naumachie*, served with a slow-cooked ragù according to owner Alfredo Micheli's grandmother's recipe. Sublime desserts include a pastry filled with chantilly cream and chocolate. A lively crew of arty types, players from Roma football club and Virtus, the local basketball team, can be seen munching here. Le Naumachie can get crowded so it is worth booking if you intend to visit during the weekend.

SHADY AND SERENE
10 Villa Celimontana
Via della Navicella

Respite from the hum-drum of city life can be found in the serene settings of Villa Celimontana, a well-tended Renaissance-style garden located in front of the church of Santo Stefano. The entrance gates are in Via della Navicella by the delightful boat-shaped fountain *Navicella* (1513), made for Pope Leo X. Formerly the Villa Mattei, Villa Celimontana was transformed in 1553 by the dukes Mattei from vineyards into classical gardens filled with palm trees and exotic botanical species. The villa has an obelisk, remnants of Roman walls and stunning views over the Circo Massimo and the 1960s FAO headquarters. Try to visit during the balmy summer nights of the music festival of Villa Celimontana, when jazz singers and musicians perform under the palm trees, filling the park with blue notes. With the performers ranging from Keith Jarrett and Lou Reed to home-grown talent Roberto Gatto, the programming is always impeccable and intriguing. The city's best clubs and bars set up temporary outposts here during the festival, attracting Rome's bright young things along with jazz connoisseurs.

CIRCLES OF BEAUTY
11 Santo Stefano Rotondo
Via di Santo Stefano Rotondo

The Church of Santo Stefano Rotondo eschews conventional notions of beauty by surprising its visitors first with its circular architecture and then with its macabre contents. Built in the 5th century on the remains of Nero's great market, the *Macellum magnum*, it originally featured three concentric naves, separated from one another by rings of antique columns. It was restored in 1453 by Pope Nicholas V who walled in the outer circle of columns thereby changing the scale of the place. On the walls thirty-four faded frescoes, painted in the 16th century by Pomarancio and Antonio Tempesta, realistically illustrate the tortures received by early Christian martyrs. From chopped hands to scalding oil treatments, the depictions are terrifying but fascinating. Next door to the church, in the secluded shady garden, is a small gardener's house deemed to be where the composer Palestrina wrote his sacred music in the 16th century, surely inspired by the celestial atmosphere.

DIVINE DEN
12 Divinare
Via Ostilia 4

Among the rowdier Roman trattorias and gladiator-themed pubs that pepper the area, this intimate wine bar is a true find for those wanting a 'quiet night out'. For years this was a local drinking den with wine straight out of the barrels and a few tables serving simple dishes to the locals. Now Divinare has transformed itself into a more sophisticated French bistro-inspired establishment, serving a wine list with over 700 crus – there are bottles stacked up to the ceiling. Light meals such as salads, carpaccios and a good cheese and cured meat selection fall into the *enoteca* formula, while excellent chocolate pralines are served with a strong espresso made from a vintage coffee machine that will charge you up for the evening ahead.

sleep • eat • drink
shop • retreat

sleep

The wave of new design boutique hotels that has recently hit Rome offers a particular variation on an indigenous theme. Somehow minimal décor was never going to make an impact on such a stunning Baroque backdrop. Visitors are now spoilt for choice, whether they check into the idiosyncratic Casa Howard, the serene and palatial setting of the Wine Academy or cool cutting-edge Ripa Hotel. Most of the hotels featured are newcomers, part of a trend in hospitality that is less reliant on a central location than past grand establishments but still provides the quintessential escape experience.

Away from the frenzy of boutique row Via del Babuino, lies Via Margutta, a peaceful pedestrian road, famous since the 1950s for being where many artists had their studios and also where film director Federico Fellini lived, although today the most interesting art is more likely to be found in the nearby auction houses than in the artists' shops that line the street.

The entrance to the Hotel Art is an exercise in restraint as you walk along a narrow path of whitewashed pebbles. The hotel's name takes its cue from the street's reputation and the works of contemporary Italian art that decorate the public areas, such as Enzo Catellani's light installation at the entrance. Inside the lobby, two futuristic white resin bubbles function as reception and office, while the old vaulted ceiling is frescoed a deep cobalt blue with golden stars. Because the building was originally a chapel and is listed as a historic building, the Roman architects Sycamore had to work hard to blend the period features with their particular style of understated design. Mixing the sacred with the profane, the marble altar is enshrined by a glass panel and located just behind the bar counter, which serves breakfasts and light meals in an area of the lobby. For heartier meals, guests are conveniently close to Margutta Vegetariano (p. 138) as well as Osteria della Frezza (p. 144).

Colour is the other theme of the hotel, and each corridor leading to the guest rooms is either blue, orange, green or yellow. On the floor, narrow light strips are etched with verses by poets Garcia Lorca and Octavio Paz. The forty-six rooms are all decently sized and combine attention to detail – bed-boards in hand-stitched leather, air conditioning, parquet floors – with an atmosphere of intimacy. The bathrooms are micro-tiled in bright colours reinforcing the chromatic link with the corridors.

14 Palazzetto at the International Wine Academy

49 Vicolo del Bottino 8
Rooms from €200

A four-storey, turn-of-the-20th-century honey-hued building perched on the Spanish Steps, the Palazzetto has just four luxurious rooms. Owned by Roberto Wirth, of nearby Hotel Hassler Villa Medici, it is a bolthole for those attending the International Wine Academy, with early evening tastings on the superbly located roof terrace. Other customers come to this townhouse hotel for its intimate surroundings and pared-down décor. Each bedroom is individually decorated with pale and neutral tones, although the beds are a display of indulgence with their printed velvet covers, linen sheets and tiers of taffeta silk pillows. The mini-bars are well stocked with Italian wines.

Guests have a number of different dining options. The wood-panelled Library provides food for thought with its impressive wine book collection; the display cases are packed with bottles from all over the world. On the first floor, the Wine bar/Salon is a more informal affair, where chef Antonio Martucci will rustle up a plate of mozzarella, Roman ham (*coppa*) or an artichoke salad. A fireplace, comfy armchairs and a chess set give the area a warm, clubby feel. In fine weather, breakfast is served in the ivy-clad garden, next to an appropriately placed statue of Bacchus.

Guests are also given their own set of keys so that they can come and go at all times via the roof terrace, and the service is relaxed, materializing only at times of need. The circular wrought-iron staircase may remind film lovers of Bertolucci's film *L'Assedio*, starring Thandy Newton, which was filmed here. Whether you wish to meander through the smart shopping streets around the Spanish Steps or just live out your own *Roman Holiday* fantasy, this is the ideal private palazzo experience.

This quirky guesthouse is actually two separate palazzi, perfectly located a stone's throw from shopping heaven, Piazza di Spagna. An intimate and luxurious Roman residence, with an attentive housekeeper, Casa Howard's owners are Jennifer Howard, originally from Britain, and her husband, Count Massimo Leonardi di Casalino. Apparently the guesthouse's name is also a play on the Italian translation of the Merchant Ivory film of E. M. Forster's novel, *Howard's End*.

The palazzo in Via di Capo Le Case has only five rooms, each with parquet floors, coffered ceilings, family oil paintings and antiques. The rooms are named after their decorative schemes: the decadent Chinese Room has fabrics sourced from Shanghai Tang in Hong Kong, while the White Room is decorated with pretty black-and-white Toile de Jouy with red trimmings. Not every room in Capo Le Case has an en suite facilities: those who must make the trip to the bathroom are supplied with dainty slippers and a kimono. A small Turkish hamman provides welcome respite after a day of sightseeing.

The second property was opened in Via Sistina in 2002. It was decorated by Rome-based designer Tommaso Ziffer, also responsible for the nearby Hotel de la Russie. Ziffer's mark can be found in the unashamedly maximalist style of the rooms, while still remaining true to the essentially cosy feel of the place. The American Cousin Room is a true bachelor pad, with large flat-screen TV, internet connection and shiny black contemporary furniture, while the Zebra Room is a sensory overload of black-and-white prints and red floors and walls. Breakfast is served in your room, with warm croissants and jam from the Leonardi's farmhouse in Tuscany. A well-stocked fridge in the hallway is there for everyone to use.

A SUPERIOR BED & BREAKFAST
46 **Relais Banchi Vecchi**
23 Via dei Banchi Vecchi 115
Rooms from €125

Finding a reasonably priced place to stay in the more historic areas of the city can be a challenge, so newcomer Relais Banchi Vecchi is a welcome addition to Rome's hospitality map. The hotel is hidden behind a solid wooden door on Via dei Banchi Vecchi, a lovely street lined with artisans' workshops and not far from Via Giulia. The official entrance is tucked away in tiny Via del Pavone. Housed in a palazzo owned by the family Sforza Cesarini, Relais Banchi Vecchi combines the intimacy of a bed and breakfast with the grandness of past Roman aristocratic life. The director, stylish former concert pianist Milena Stojkovic, runs the place like clockwork and will arrange anything from booking a car to the airport to meals out.

The multilayered history of the building is evident in the small but atmospheric rooms – exposed Roman masonry, medieval beams, coconut wood floors and large windows overlooking either Via dei Banchi Vecchi or the courtyard off Vicolo del Pavone. Bathrooms are spacious with marble-topped basins and terracotta tiled floors. The furnishings are unfussy – draped red curtains, embroidered bedspreads and a couple of 19th-century antique chairs are as far as it goes. On the walls, Piranesi's prints of ancient Roman ruins are appropriate adornments. This isn't a glamorous hotel, but it has an authenticity that is charming and in a superb location. Bonus points come from it being next door to top drinking den Il Goccetto (p. 56) as well as cheap and cheerful restaurant Boccondivino (p. 24).

Before the arrival of the Aleph, ES (now the Radisson SAS) and Art hotels, the Ripa was the only aesthetically challenging hotel to be found in Rome, patronized by design-conscious travellers. Fast-forward a couple of years and Jeremy King and Riccardo Roselli's boldly designed hotel still holds its own, thanks to a successful blend of futuristic forms and comfortable, pared-down environments. Grey and white toned bedrooms have pebble-patterned carpets, ample beds and no closet space, so that guests' clothes are on display. The all-white 1960s-inspired curvaceous bathrooms are functionally high tech and stylish. The look is a far cry from the more conventional gilded and decorative Roman options, but then the clientele is not your average crowd. Party people love to check in at the new presidential suite, room 806, with its cocoon-shaped silver and white sleeping area, two balconies and an unashamedly large jacuzzi.

At the 150-seat 'risto-bar' Riparte Café guests sit on blonde timber chairs to sample a sophisticated and light menu created with produce from the proprietors' farm, Le Roscioline. The atmosphere in the bar is decidedly warmer as the terracotta and white walls are covered with displays of contemporary art and the floors and panelling are decked out in dark wood. Next door, Suite (p. 70) is one of the city's favourite addresses for discerning clubbers. Although officially still in Trastevere, Ripa's location is off the beaten track, and has a view of high-rise concrete blocks rather than of Baroque churches. But it is convenient for Porta Portese flea market (p. 70) and just a short stroll away from the historic heart of the city.

SEVENTH HEAVEN

14 **Aleph Hotel**
73 Via di San Basilio 15
Rooms from €350

'A journey filled with heavenly places and sinful delights' is how American designer Adam Tihany describes the hotel that he created for the Boscolo Group in 2003. Tihany, who was also responsible for restaurants Le Cirque 2000 in New York and Foliage in London, has created the Aleph in his signature lavish style, combining contemporary design with sensuous overtones. It is one of Rome's most atmospheric boltholes, a place to get lost in for a couple of hours, or even days. Popular with the most glamorous Italians, Emanuele Filiberto, son of the exiled heir to the throne, chose it for his wedding reception.

A strong heaven-and-hell theme dominates the public areas. Guests entering the black-and-red lobby are greeted by two over-sized replica samurai, while a plasma screen plays back a video of their entry. Rich red drapery conceals mysterious dark corners, and huge white sofas are a focal point for the black-clad staff, on call to satisfy your every whim. A giant bell hangs from the ceiling, and in the courtyard dangle two sculptural dice, an ironic reminder of the perils of falling into temptation.

In the guest rooms the emphasis is on relaxation, with blue and cream tones, and black-and-white images of Roman street scenes photographed by Tihany's son, Bram. There are Murano glass chandeliers and window blinds made from strings of metal beads. In addition, there are six suites that represent complete indulgence, with bathrooms in onyx marble, private roof terraces and outdoor jacuzzis. The hotel was formerly a bank, and a giant safe downstairs has been converted into a relaxation room: you will find it next door to the small Paradise spa room.Tucked just behind Via Vittorio Veneto, the road immortalized in Federico Fellini's film *La Dolce Vita*, the Aleph seems to have kick-started a small design renaissance in the area.

TRAINSPOTTER'S DELIGHT

92 **Radisson SAS**

12
Via Filippo Turati 171
Rooms from €160

Glimpsed from a train entering Rome's Termini station, the Radisson SAS's curvaceous silhouette is a surprising addition to the city's skyline of placid Baroque domes and TV aerials. The seven-storey modernist building would not look out of place in a metropolis like London or New York, yet it has its own Mediterranean flavour, aided by the top-floor decked roof terrace, with its blue micro-tiled swimming pool and stunning views of the Frascati hills. Formerly the ES Hotel, it is the creation of King & Roselli, the Anglo–Italian team behind the boutique Ripa Hotel in Trastevere, and it was originally owned by the Roscioli family. It is located in the Esquilino area, Rome's most up-and-coming neighbourhood.

Enter the vast lobby and you are greeted by a luminescent reception desk and Cappellini benches by Jean-Marie Massaud. While all 235 rooms feature exquisite design details, the twenty-seven suites are particularly geared towards the cosmopolitan traveller: ingenious ideas include a bed that folds up to leave space for a meeting room, a bathtub and sleeping area separated only by a curtain, and private terraces decorated with olive trees and Jasper Morrison's Thinking Man chairs. On the seventh floor, the restaurant Sette features an open kitchen, a grand polished wood counter and chairs by Sawaya & Moroni. Glass doors lead to the roof terrace dominated by its swimming pool, which is accessible to non-guests via a special membership scheme. The Zest bar (p. 99) opens up to views of the recently restored Termini station, built in the 1930s by Angiolo Mazzoni. During the construction of the hotel various historical remains were unearthed, and the entrance is now shared with an excavation area, which is due to become an archaeological site and part of the regeneration scheme for Esquilino.

106 **Hotel Capo d'Africa**

8 Via Capo d'Africa 54
Rooms from €270

Until a few years ago staying at a hotel near the Colosseum would have been an unexciting choice, but since the Celio neighbourhood has been reinvented as a buzzing area, residents at the Hotel Capo d'Africa can happily benefit from a profusion of good quality restaurants and bars. The hotel has had some star guests – writer Banana Yoshimoto and Nobel prize-winner John Coetzee stayed here during Rome's literature festival, and Lou Reed and Laurie Anderson held a few memorable parties on the terrace of their suite after performing at the nearby Villa Celimontana jazz festival (p. 113).

Designed by British architect Harry Gregory of ARA Design, the hotel manages to combine a design-conscious soul with vernacular touches. Dating from 1900, the ochre tinted building was previously a convent and retains original features like the wrought-iron staircase and old stone steps. The public areas have high ceilings and the walls are lined with art and installations by Italian artists such as Paolo Canevari and Mariano Rossano. In the spacious lobby some notable Artemide lamps are set among blueberry-hued sofas by Antonio Bonacina; the wicker chairs create a pleasant, airy atmosphere. Next door to the glass and marble reception counter is the open bar Centrum, specializing in whiskies and cigars but also serving appropriately named Caput Mundi and Colosseum cocktails.

The sixty-five rooms are different sizes and understated in their décor. Ochre, saffron and sand are the warm tones employed throughout, with stylish touches like the blonde wood headrest on the beds, red leather armchairs and bathrooms decorated with stucco. The views from the sunny breakfast hall on the top floor are stunning and overlook the Celio, the Colosseum and the Parco Oppio. In the evening, linger on the terrace with its lemon trees in terracotta pots, climbing roses and silvery olive tree.

eat

Rome's cuisine has moved on from its gutsy, simple origins of *cucina povera* (rustic cooking) and now offers some of the best restaurants in Italy. Blessed with first-rate produce, from sun-kissed vegetables to fresh fish from the nearby coast, the cuisine is all about flavours rather than elaborate techniques. A young generation of chefs and restaurateurs is promoting a return to traditional dishes cooked with a twist, and attention is focused on food with a traceable origin and sourced from small-batch producers. It remains, however, the traditional *hosterie* and *trattorias* that hold strong in the hearts and stomachs of most Romans.

46 **L'Altro di Mastai**

27 Via Giovanni Giraud 53

Fabio Baldassare, the chef at L'Altro di Mastai, is a star in the making. He has already worked with Heinz Beck, the creative mind behind the Michelin-starred La Pergola at the Rome Hilton Hotel, and with Raymond Blanc at Le Manoir aux Quat'Saisons in Oxford. L'Altro di Mastai is in the hotspot behind Piazza Navona. Dress glamorous if you want to blend in with the precise, formal service and luxurious interior of soft yellows and deep reds. Fabio's cooking belongs to the school of innovative Italian cuisine, and the menu changes every couple of months according to seasonal produce. Most dishes are small but intensely flavoured. A tender swordfish fillet is teamed up with cauliflower purée, orange sauce and marinated sea bass eggs, while spaghetti is tossed with a moist sauce of wild asparagus and shrimps. Home-baked bread and pastries, petit fours, and a cheese trolley for the end of meal diehards, will guarantee a most satisfactory experience. The cellar is impressive – let the sommelier guide you through the 1000 Italian and French labels.

SMOOTH OPERATOR

64 **Antico Arco**

3 Piazzale Aurelio 7

Perched on top of the Gianicolo hill, just behind the arch of San Pancrazio, Antico Arco can be reached via one of the most evocative climbs in Rome. Once there, you are rewarded by the calm, cool atmosphere, friendly welcome and food to die for. Owners Patrizia Mattei, Domenico Calio and Maurizio Minore all come from a non-restaurant background, but they have turned Antico Arco into an essential destination. The menu takes its cue from fresh, seasonal ingredients, which are transformed into ingenious combinations. A Roman classic like cheese and pepper (cacio e pepe) spaghetti is teamed up with a sauce made from courgette flowers, while a lobster and tiger prawn warm salad is tossed over gazpacho and Thai rice. The interior design, by local architect Tatà Gallo, features neutral tones and bespoke furniture. The impressive wine cellar boasts 1200 labels from around the world, and you can order by the glass at the small bar by the entrance.

64 **San Teodoro**
32 Via dei Fienili 49–51

Tucked away in a medieval street off Via San Teodoro, with its seamless views of the Forum, this little corner of Rome has a quiet stillness that gives a real sense of times past. But San Teodoro's owner, Giorgio Cialone, is not one to rest on his laurels and he works hard to create a temple to sophisticated Mediterranean cooking. The décor is a pleasant combination of brick-vaulted ceilings, airy archways and terracotta-hued walls. Abstract art and artful flower installations give the place a chic but warm atmosphere. For the perfect romantic date, try for the decked patio outside – on balmy summer nights you'll be seduced by the wafts of scent from the nearby climbing jasmine. Among chef Luciano Zaza's dishes are succulent spaghetti with shrimps, shavings of *pecorino di fossa* and courgette flowers, mouth-melting octopus carpaccio with peppers, red onion-stuffed ravioli and seared tuna with pancetta. The wine list is impeccable, as is the service.

FIFTH QUARTER CUISINE
80 **Checchino dal 1887**
14 Via di Monte Testaccio 30

The brothers Mariani run this elegant bistro-style restaurant, providing customers with a top wine list and a traditional Roman menu that reads like the anatomy of a cow. In Checchino dal 1887, named after their grandfather Francesco, you can sample the cuisine of *il quinto quarto*, the fifth quarter, named after the top-up wage given to the workers at the nearby slaughterhouse. Offal, heads, oxtails and hooves are among the ingredients of this gutsy cuisine. For the faint-hearted there are also more delicate dishes, such as *saltimbocca alla romana* (veal with ham and sage) or *agnello alla cacciatora* (lamb sautéed with chilli and red wine). The restaurant's cellars, housed inside the Testaccio's Monte dei Cocci (a hill created during ancient Roman times of countless pieces of broken amphorae; p. 81), are worth a visit as the brothers pride themselves on being lovers of prestigious French and Italian labels.

14 Margutta Vegetariano

45 Via Margutta 118

Gastronomic Romans can be very conventional about food; they like the traditional sequence of a first course of pasta and a second course of meat. But Claudio Vanini's vegetarian restaurant, the first ever to be opened in Rome, has managed to convert even the most ferocious of meat eaters. The secret is, of course, in the cooking: tender vegetable balls in tomato sauce, crunchy brown rice with ginger, fragrant broad beans and cauliflower terrine, followed by delicious desserts such as lemon cream with fruit berries. The décor creates a good atmosphere, with vividly coloured walls and some reasonable art. Pop in for brunch and seat yourself at one of the large bay windows where you can observe the antiquarians and artists that work on this picturesque street.

46 Cul de Sac

39 Piazza di Pasquino 73

More of an eye opener than a dead end, this Cul de Sac offers a mouth-watering selection of 1500 wines, served with an impressive assortment of cold cuts, patés, cheeses, warm soups and pasta. This delightful, small *enoteca*, which has been around since 1977, is all snug banquette seating and marble counter with travel racks of wines overhead to give it a retro feel. Lunchtime is when Cul de Sac has the most buzz, although it also attracts a youngish dinner crowd. The food is fresh and satisfying though not made on the premises. The Greek salad glistens, the smoked swordfish is on the right side of salty and the north Italian taleggio cheese oozes from its skin. The wines are the stars, and the staff are on hand to recommend the best pairings, featuring vintages from Piedmont and Tuscany as well as Bordeaux, though do try the best from the nearby vineyards of Lazio. A final freshly brewed espresso makes the afternoon's activities a more acceptable proposition.

RENEWED CLASSIC
Hostaria dell'Orso

44 Via dei Soldati 25c

Hosteria dell'Orso is strikingly located in a medieval tower, just off Piazza Navona overlooking the River Tiber. Inside, faded frescoes blend with contemporary touches like the bright red seating. For many years dining at Hosteria dell'Orso was a formal experience, but all that changed when Milanese star chef Gualtiero Marchesi (who also has establishments in Paris, Milan and L'Alberetta on the Italian Lakes) took over with his trademark tweaking of Italian classics. However, it's his talented disciple Fabrizio Molteni's cooking that steals the show. A melon juice with shrimp wrapped in ham as a starter is followed by risotto with saffron and fillet of veal Rossini. For fish, try the *gran piatto di pesce*, a selection of salmon with dill, baby squid, scallops with ginger and sublime cold spaghetti tossed in a caviar sauce. Desserts include a surprising *semifreddo* with black pepper and honey or a meringue cake. Sommelier Kan Oya will guide you through the wine list, but expect a high mark-up. Reservations should be made at least two weeks in advance.

TRASTEVERE'S BEST
Enoteca Ferrara

8 Piazza Trilussa 41

Enoteca Ferrara knocks spots off the multitude of mediocre establishments in Trastevere. This restaurant, wine bar and delicatessen occupies the whole corner building between Piazza Trilussa and Via del Moro. Converted from a former convent, its style is eclectic. A bridged walkway overhangs the vaulted, all-white basement while the dining rooms offer a succession of different decorative schemes. A highlight is the delightful wisteria-clad courtyard. Sisters Lina and Maria run the place with some flair, the first as an established sommelier (there are 850 wines to choose from) and the second as a cook who knows how to play with tradition. A typical evening kicks off with fish soup with Vesuvio cherry tomatoes, stewed rabbit and swordfish rolls. In the summer, the few outdoor chairs make it an ideal spot for an *aperitivo*. On the counter is a selection of *stuzzichini*: morsels of pizza, fried polenta, cold cuts of ham and olives, which function as *stuzzicare* to whet your appetite.

46 Roscioli

Coming from a family of bakers, Alessandro and Pierluigi Roscioli's latest venture is an *alimentari* (deli) that is also a wine bar at lunchtime and a restaurant in the evening. The shop counter has beautifully stacked goodies from all over Italy: juicy hams from Parma, fresh ricotta from the neighbouring countryside, and huge shapes of *caciocchiato*, a cheese they buy in the Irpinia region and then season in their own caves in the Marche for another four months. Roscioli stocks most of Italy's established wine producers as well as an inspiring selection of balsamic vinegars and extra virgin olive oils. Customers can sample everything before buying and are given advice about possible wine and food combinations. Better still they can retreat to the back room to taste the superb dishes that chef Paolo conjures up. Firm favourites are the broad-bean and mushroom soup served with pecorino cheese, stuffed celery with fondue, foie gras with grilled pears and marsala sauce and, to top it all, the famous *cappuccino di ricotta*, which is pure bliss.

64 Alberto Ciarla

Glass fish sculptures, deep-red velvet sofas and a long black lacquer bar set the tone at Alberto Ciarla, Rome's best bet for fresh fish. But the jaw-dropping 1970s décor is no preparation for Alberto Ciarla's subtle and refined menu. Alberto is from a well-known family of restaurateurs and wine producers from the Castelli region outside Rome. He opened his Trastevere restaurant in 1974. Long before Rome's current fascination with sushi, Ciarla excelled at raw fish recipes (*crudi di pesce*), something learnt during his travels in Peru and Japan. Roman tradition also features strongly, such as his *fritto antico*, a dish of deep-fried semolina covered baby squid, calamari and prawns, apparently adapted from Pope Pius V's chef's cookbook. From the three- or four-course tasting menus, pick the *grande cucina* for lobster and langoustines, the Tyrrhenian Sea inspired one for seafood and bean soup, and sea bass fillet with aromatic herbs, or the raw one for all types of delectable fish carpaccios.

LOUCHE LOUNGE

46 **Supperclub**
45 Via dei Nari 14

Like its sister club in Amsterdam, Supperclub offers a plush lounge/dining/club experience, attracting a mix of savvy foreigners and local partygoers. Set in a grand 18th-century palazzo in the cobbled, medieval Via dei Nari hidden in the dark streets behind the Pantheon, Supperclub does its own modernist spin on Roman decadence. Vernacular beams and vaulted frescoed ceilings punch through two levels of clean white space. The vibe is self-indulgent as guests kick off their shoes to recline on pristine white sofas. Dinner is a five-course fusion-style menu, with DJ Marco Moreggia's rare groove soundtrack in the background. A shiatsu masseur is on call for further relaxation. After dinner, the sound system revs up for deep house, guest singers perform Salsoul dance classics, and there's entertainment from the club's resident transvestite. After 11 p.m. Supperclub throws its doors open to themed club nights and special events.

14 **La Campana**
31 Vicolo della Campana 18

La Campana claims to be Rome's oldest restaurant – food was served from these premises as long ago as 1518. According to Livio Janattoni, an authority on the history of Roman food (and author of many cookbooks), this was the queen of the city's trattorias, where hospitality and good home cooking reigned supreme. Today's restaurant keeps it simple – white-linen tablecloths are paired with bistro-style dark wood chairs and a few prints of the city on the walls. The food does much of the talking. In springtime, try *vignarola*, a rich stew made from broad beans, artichokes, peas and pancetta and *saltimbocca*, veal cutlets wrapped with sage and ham. As in most Roman establishments, there is a daily special – gnocchi on Thursday, tripe on Saturday and roasted milk-fed lamb with potatoes on Sunday. For something special, take your pick from the fresh fish displayed in the window and choose how you want it to be cooked.

14 **La Rosetta**
11 Via della Rosetta 8

Since opening forty years ago, La Rosetta has been a mecca for fish: it was the first restaurant in Rome to serve it exclusively on the menu. If imitation is the best form of flattery this is clearly proved by all the other restaurants that have adopted many of La Rosetta's recipes, such as the ubiquitous warm salad of rocket and prawns. Massimo Riccioli is the celebrated talent behind La Rosetta's constant success. Charming and unpretentious, Massimo compares his inventive cooking to a jam session, 'an act of improvisation where fresh materials are cooked into delectable combinations'. The results include tuna tartare, baby squid and mushy peas, homemade pasta with aubergine, grouper, black olives and sea bass cooked under a coarse crust. A French pastry cook bakes chocolate cakes and other delicious sweets, while the service is a master class in discretion and professionalism. The pricey menu means that this is largely a haunt of the more wealthy among us.

64 Sora Lella

17 Via di Ponte Quattro Capi 16

Wedged between the Trastevere and the old Jewish Ghetto is the peaceful and secluded island of Tiberina, which for gourmets is a site of pilgrimage thanks to the presence of Sora Lella, one of the city's most celebrated (and pricey) establishments. Sora Lella was the sister of Roman actor Aldo Fabrizi, star of Neo-Realist cinema, including Roberto Rossellini's masterpiece, *Roma Città Aperta*. She was a formidable cook and an occasional actress; her son Aldo Trabalza later took over the restaurant, which is housed in a medieval tower with a view of the Tiber. Unfussy and unpretentious dishes reveal a refined artistry of taste with a talent for reinvention. A recent winter visit started with the house speciality *tonnarelli alla cuccagna* (pasta with sausage pancetta and nuts), *maialino in agrodolce Antica Roma* (a tasty roast suckling pig in a sweet-and-sour sauce with prunes, pine nuts and raisins), steamed salt cod on a soft bed of potato mash, and Aldo's scrumptious ricotta cake with bitter chocolate.

46 Al Bric

14 Via del Pellegrino 51–52

Taking the *enoteca* concept to new heights, Al Bric provides a cool and calm atmosphere in which to savour a divine wine list (the French are top of the list here, but space is also given to important producers from Tuscany and Piedmont) with the sophisticated flavours of a menu that is divided into dishes of the sea and land. Among Al Bric's signature dishes are spaghetti with prawns, figs and roquefort cheese, a beef tartare with parmesan and a coulis of rocket, and a stroganoff of swordfish with thyme and squid. Wine labels decorate the walls, and the owner's wife has even created trompe l'oils in celebration of Château Margaux. The formidable cheese selection is displayed in the window, and you can choose tastings from the the Italian and French varieties to eat with fragrant breadsticks baked on the premises. A good selection of grappas, dessert wines, whiskies, calvados and cognacs ensure the evening ends on a high note.

Not content with just owning Gusto next door – a 300-seat eaterie specializing in contemporary Italian food – the Tudini family opened Osteria della Frezza, a smaller, brasserie-style restaurant whose menu is a modernized take on Roman cuisine. Chef Marco Gallotta runs both restaurants but has a particular attachment to La Frezza, where he rustles up classics like *polpette al sugo* (meatballs with tomato sauce) or *rigatoni alla matriciana* (pasta with a spicy bacon sauce). La Frezza's main claim to culinary fame is having introduced the notion of *cicchetto*, a selection of small dishes like tapas. Depending on what the kitchen is preparing, waiters will suggest a series of dainty portions of pasta, meat or vegetables to give customers a varied eating experience. A further temptation is the cheese board, custom prepared in the see-through cheese room built in a corner of the dining hall. With over 200 types sourced from Italy and France, it is hardly surprising that the restaurant employs a cheese master to turn them regularly and check their temperature (seven degrees) or level of seasoning. Leather banquettes, wooden stairways, and vintage black-and-white photography create a warm and comfortable environment.

A few intimate tables are what you find at Agata e Romeo, semi-hidden behind the majestic basilica of Santa Maria Maggiore. Inside, the décor is reassuringly understated, perhaps to focus attention on the much-applauded Roman cuisine of Agata Parisello. A cookery writer, teacher and broadcaster as well as talented chef, Agata's passion for traditional Roman cuisine and her desire to update it through constant experimentation has become a blueprint for a younger generation of chefs in the city. Originally an *osteria*, where only wine would be served, then a trattoria, Agata took over the restaurant from her father in 1980. She runs it with her husband, Romeo, one of Rome's more knowledgeable sommeliers. Since then, Agata e Romeo's success story has been consistently sanctioned by the best food guides, and rightly so. Be prepared to be surprised by the delicate oxtail and celery terrine, the *cacio e pepe* (cheese and pepper) pasta made with Sicilian saffron cheese, and her speciality, *millefoglie al cucchiaio*, millefeuille with a rich, runny cream.

14 **Baba**

87 Via Casale di Tor di Quinto 1

You will need a taxi to get there but it is well worth the inconvenience and expense for a truly original experience. Set in a tiny medieval hamlet, not far from Renzo Piano's Auditorium (p. 42), the building is an old *casolare* – a traditional farmhouse with outdoor patio. Baba is the larger-than-life character who is the soul of the restaurant – a formidable cook as much as a raconteur, and the most gracious host. Arrive before nine o'clock and seat yourself at one of the few tables so that you do not miss Baba's ringing of the bell to kick off dinner. She will explain the regional origin of the dishes, which are all prepared with organic vegetables. The very reasonable fixed-price menu offers two seasonal soups and then a buffet-style selection of wholesome dishes, such as gnocchi pasta with courgettes, veal meatballs, and risotto with melon and ham. The restaurant is only open for dinner, and a reservation of a least a week ahead is essential.

NO FRILLS TRATTORIA

92 **Uno e Bino**

8 Via degli Equi 58 —

Unlike its high-brow name, a play on a semiotic study of *Pinocchio*, Uno e Bino is rather unpretentious. Set up by brother and sister Gianpaolo and Gloria Gravina in 1997, this establishment is part of the *enoteca* movement that has changed the city's gastronomic map for the better. A well-researched wine list (try any wine from Sicilian producer Planeta) goes hand in hand with the homely and imaginative food. Uno e Bino's menu changes seasonally, but classics that are always available include *paccheri* pasta with pork sauce and marjoram ricotta, braised beef cheeks with cocoa and red wine, stewed salt cod with crunchy potatoes and lentil cream, and chef Andrea Buscema's divine *tortino di cioccolato*. Unlike its trendier San Lorenzo neighbours, Uno e Bino does not do super cool interior design – dark wood tables with waxed paper coverings and wine guides lining the bookshelves give it a casual feel – but it's a little gem not to be overlooked.

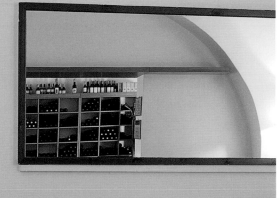

SICILIAN CHIC

14 **Trattoria** —

21 Via del Pozzo delle Cornacchie 25

Chef Filippo La Mantia manages to combine enviable culinary skills with a knack for socializing with Rome's celebrity circles. A self-taught cook, La Mantia was a photographic reporter until he decided to leave his native Sicily and try his fortune in Rome. His new kingdom is Trattoria, a stylish den of sleek contemporary design by architects Marco and Gianluigi Giammetta, located on the top floor of a building not far from San Luigi dei Francesi (p. 23). From his open-to-view kitchen La Mantia prepares Sicilian classics updated for the modern palate – his *caponata* (a sweet-and-sour stew of aubergines) is cooked with no added oil, garlic or onion and is delightfully light. Rigatoni with a pesto of almonds, capers, anchovies and breadcrumbs; tuna with a couscous of zesty lemons and oranges; and, of course, Sicily's most famous sweet, *la cassata*, an ice cream peppered with candied fruit, are among the menu's offerings. The wine list is heavily inclined towards Sicily as are the cheeses (from Ragusa) and the wide choice of olive oils.

drink

Coffee and wine are what quenches this city's thirst. A cappuccino in the morning is Rome's most rooted ritual, and one that very few bars get wrong. A more recent trend are the *enoteche*, wine bars that focus on Italian producers, often serving innovative yet rustic food. The *enoteca* formula shook Rome's drinking map in the early 1980s and was largely represented by a team of wine enthusiasts who opened places like Bleve and Cul de Sac in the Piazza Navona area. Around midnight, drinking in the new breed of design clubs and bars becomes a more libertine affair as the cautious tendency to pair alcohol with food fades and the real fun begins.

 46 **Il Simposio**

47 Piazza Cavour 16

Costantini is one of Rome's better-stocked wine shops. It also has a tiny wine bar that doubles as restaurant Il Simposio at the back. This is not a place that thrives on passing trade; only those in the know appreciate the intricately crafted Art Déco metalwork throughout and the slightly old-fashioned feel. Gianni Ruggiero is the knowledgeable sommelier in charge, and you can sample around thirty wine labels listed on a chalk board at the counter. The food at the restaurant is also pretty good,

with Piedmontese chef Alessandro Mora serving classic Italian fare like a lobster salad with oranges, or sea bass with fennel and shallots. But it is the 260-bottle cellar downstairs that, arguably, is its strongest asset. The nearby Law Courts provide a clientele of lawyers, judges and solicitors, while in the evening the dark and plush atmosphere of the restaurant works wonders as a setting for romantic dinners.

Bar della Pace
35 Via della Pace 4–7

 Il Bicchiere di Mastai
28 Via dei Banchi Nuovi 52

Seasons may come and go but the Bar della Pace's reputation as one of Rome's sexiest bars remains. Framed by a wonderful climbing vine, the bar sits on the corner of Via della Pace, just next door to the Bramante's beautiful cloister (p. 60). La Pace's interiors are dark and cool, with Art Déco statues, large mirrors and vases overflowing with decadent lilies. During the day the bar is a local café, but after dinner it comes into its own, serving cocktails to the young crowd spilling into the street.

Located opposite its grander sister restaurant L'Altro di Mastai (p. 136) Il Bicchiere di Mastai is more affordable and has a very different atmosphere. Try the locally produced spicy red Falesco or Castel De Paolis's superb Villa Adriana, a blend of Malvasia and Viognier. Excellent food is guaranteed by Fabio Baldessarre's kitchen – fresh cod on a bed of warm carpaccio of tomatoes is one of his specialities. On Thursdays, wine producers from all over Italy come here to extol the virtue of their wines as part of a set menu and wine tasting event.

14 Caffè Tazza D'Oro
10 Via degli Orfani 84

The 1950s kitschy décor of Tazza D'Oro – all wood panelling, African-inspired bas-reliefs, coffee sacks and a very un-PC naked black lady (a logo designed by an architect staying at the American Academy) – makes this café worth a visit. But what really elevates it to a site of pilgrimage among coffee addicts is the pungent aroma wafting from this ancient *torrefazione* (coffee-grinder). Tazza D'Oro's own blend, called La Regina dei Caffè, is a strong mix of Arabic beans and creates a powerful espresso. Another speciality is the sweet *granita di caffè* (frozen coffee crushed into a velvety slushlike ice and served in a glass between layers of whipped cream). The café also sells chocolate-covered coffee beans and a coffee liqueur.

WINE EMPORIUM
14 Casa Bleve
17 Via del Teatro Valle 48–49

Anacleto Bleve knows a thing or two about wine – for years he ran his tiny shop in the Old Jewish Ghetto (p. 74), effectively spearheading the *enoteca* movement in Rome. Now that he has moved to more palatial premises – a 14th-century converted coach house in front of the Teatro Valle – he can afford to indulge in equally grand crus. From super Tuscan red Sassicaia to Trentino's Saint Michel's Epan Sauvignon, the excellence of Italian producers really shines. The high ceilings, arches and restored wooden stable doors provide an airy ambience, while faux Roman statues, including a Bacchus and a marble fountain, set the mood for a light lunch from the cold buffet or a glass (or two) after dinner. Downstairs, remnants of a Roman wall are visible as well as two cellars packed with covetable wine labels.

For a taste of old-style grandeur pop into Caffè Greco to sample a *caffè con panna* (coffee with cream) in one of the more intimate back rooms. The environment oozes faded charm, with its marble-topped circular tables, deep red velvet banquettes and precious mosaic floors. There are framed letters on the walls, marble busts and Art Déco statuettes, as well as Grand Tour–inspired panoramic views of the Eternal City. This historic café has been the favourite haunt of literary and artistic circles since it opened in 1742. Goethe, Byron and Schopenhauer were among its illustrious patrons, coming here to sample the 'magic' drink newly imported from America. The café reached the peak of its popularity in the 1800s – aristocrats joined bohemians to philosophize about life. Like all bastions of past civilization, today Caffè Greco attracts a mixture of curious sightseers as well as suited businessmen rather than intellectual circles, but it is still worth a viewing.

Sant'Eustachio's décor, which includes bas-reliefs of plantation life, coffee sacks and diagrams, reveals this café's dedication to the art of coffee making. Indeed, Sant'Eustachio's *gran caffè* blend is so secret that the barman prepares it behind a partition, so that you can hear him stirring but cannot see what he's doing. Since its invention in 1938, customers have debated what makes this coffee so special, and while many myths have spread around town, the reason is probably the blend, which is made from different South American beans. Despite the groups of tourists that sometimes queue outside, this speciality – essentially a creamy and frothy cappuccino without the milk – is worth the wait. Named after the Roman general Eustace, who paid for his conversion to Catholicism by being martyred by roasting, Sant'Eustachio is run by Raimondo and Roberto Ricci, who also sell Sant'Eustachio honey, biscuits, chocolates and coffee to try at home.

CIOCCOLATE

TEA ROOM

APERITIVI

SANDWICHES

ALL DAY BAR

14 Caffè Romano
63 Hotel d'Inghilterra, Via Borgognona 4

Ladies who lunch, exhausted shoppers and ethnic food enthusiasts flock to the recently renovated Caffè Romano, located inside the Hotel d'Inghilterra, for a quick bite, an *aperitivo* or a digestive at any time of day or night. Dark wood panelling, a terracotta-toned vaulted ceiling and broad columns create an elegant and understated environment. Each dish on the cosmopolitan menu is made with authentic recipes from the world's different culinary traditions, including India and Japan. But chef Rodolfo Chieroni is also happy to rustle up Rome's speciality *cacio e pepe* (cheese and pepper), famously sampled by Woody Allen. The Caffè Romano stays open until late for dinner as well as serving as a night-cap haunt for the guests of the hotel.

A RAW APPROACH

46 Crudo
2 Via degli Specchi 6

Sultry Mediterranean beauties, boys about town and artistic types love this recently opened bar and restaurant. The name derives from the menu's raw food approach, which means morsels of sushi or cold cuts of hams served as appetizers with drinks, or a more serious – and pricey – Japanese-meets-Mediterranean menu for the upstairs restaurant (think sashimi, sushi and fish and meat carpaccio). Crudo's spacious location – it is housed on three floors of a 16th-century palazzo – meant that its owners could indulge in some serious interior decorations. The bar area features a mix of bespoke pieces. Turinese designer Michele Peretto painted the wall murals above the bar counter as well as supervising the colour schemes and decorations throughout. In the vaulted area downstairs, a small wine bar with a formidable international and Italian wine list will quench even the most demanding thirst.

46 Bar del Fico
34 Piazza del Fico 24–25

Under the benevolent shade of a fig tree that grows defiantly out of the cobblestones, this bar has been through several generations of managers down the years, but still retains its kudos as one of the historic centre's liveliest drinking dens. Inside the dark rooms are a rickety mix of thrift finds, old cinema posters on the walls and a few Art Déco touches like the marble bar counter. From spring well into October, the preened youth of Rome spill out into the tiny square for an early evening prosecco, or later for a G&T. In the afternoon, the bar has a slow paced, neighbourhood vibe, with local residents playing tournaments of chess. The faded façade of the bar has been scaffolded since the building collapsed ten years ago. Nothing has been done to restore it, which fits well with the laid-back spirit of the bar.

DESIGNER DRINKING
14 Riccioli Cafe
23 Piazza delle Coppelle 10a

This is Massimo Riccioli's – of La Rosetta (p. 142) restaurant fame – funkier outpost: a lounge bar, tea room and restaurant specializing in top sushi and oysters. Fish comes from the suppliers of La Rosetta and is always expertly prepared in front of you. Open from breakfast until 1 a.m., Riccioli caters to a discerning crowd – trendy shoppers by day and beautiful prosecco-sipping locals by night. Renaissance vaults prop up the ceiling, while the walls are covered with blue neon installations (by Massimo himself). The blue and red theme is carried across the velvet furniture, steel bar counters and funky lamps. During happy hour, the outside covered lounge area provides a vantage point for people spotting. This is a great bar to start an evening.

46 **Bloom**

38 Via Teatro Pace 30

Not far from Piazza Navona, Bloom is one of the city's most beautiful bars and fusion restaurants. Owner Dario Jacobelli has carefully overseen the styling of the place, which sports an ultra-modern style inside an ancient Roman palazzo. The menu follows the city's current fascination with sushi and is impeccably executed. The sushi bar on the first floor serves a wide range of sashimi, sushi, rigiri and the Bloom special selection, all made with very fresh fish. At the restaurant downstairs there is *orecchiette* with dried cod roe and sea urchins, and prawns sautéed with Colonnata lard and mashed chick peas. A favourite among the city's twenty-somethings this is a place to come after 11 p.m. for a post-prandial drink. Mondays is Bloomonday, a special event to which you are invited only via mobile-phone text message. The selective entry means that even well-known celebrities may not get in if they are sporting a scruffy dress code. Young, pretty models and local Latin lovers play the dating game here until late.

46 **La Vineria Reggio**

13 Piazza Campo de' Fiori 15

La Vineria could live off its location alone, perched as it is on the edge of the bustling Campo dei Fiori which, during the day, is one of Rome's oldest fruit and vegetable markets. The outdoor tables that spill onto the square provide a perfect viewpoint for people spotting, but they are snapped up fast. Run by the Reggio family for over thirty years, La Vineria has evolved from an edgy wine bar in the 1970s, frequented by local bohemians and the odd, alcoholic celebrity like Beat poet Gregory Corso, into one of the most popular destinations of the city. At sunset, Rome's tanned and beautiful youth flock here for an early evening *aperitivo*, while later in the evening the atmosphere becomes rowdier as the music is turned up. There is an extensive selection of wines by the glass, and the cellar is priced affordably enough to function as a wine shop for locals. The Reggio family also produce a very good own brand of Prosecco Conegliano.

Bar San Calisto

10 Piazza di San Calisto

Leaving the square of Santa Maria in Trastevere and heading towards the market square of Piazza San Cosimato, the surroundings gradually shed their picture perfect image to acquire the rougher feel that defined the area before foreigners and wealthy Romans moved in. Trastevere inhabitants call themselves the 'real Romans' and their cheerful, sometimes noisy attitude to life comes alive in this tiny corner bar, just next to the Arch of San Calisto. The bar goes through different transformations during the day: in the morning Roman matrons and shopkeepers have their breakfast cappuccino and *cornetto* on the outside metal tables; later, an assortment of locals, buskers and frankly shady types hang out, vaguely waiting for something to happen; while in the evening a younger crowd steps in, ordering the bar's celebrated homemade ice cream and drinking perched on the parked cars. Edgy, but fun.

TOAST OF THE TOWN

 Tazio

78 Piazza della Repubblica 47

Named after Tazio Secchiaroli, the photographer who inspired Fellini's paparazzo character in *La Dolce Vita*, the Tazio champagne bar injects a well-needed dose of glamour into the arcades that surround Piazza della Repubblica. Today the square – also known as Piazza Esedra – has been regenerated, with newly restored 19th-century palazzi offsetting the central *Fontana della Naiadi* and the ancient Baths of Diocletian. Although designed by Adam Tihany as part of the Exedra Boscolo Hotel next door, Tazio maintains its separate identity as a sophisticated drinking den thanks to its distinctively different décor. The rosewood-coffered ceiling, columns and oversized crystal chandeliers create a clubby, dark atmosphere, while 1960s photos by Secchiaroli reinforce the theme. Try one of the numerous international champagne labels and pair it with snacks from the bar menu that includes fresh oysters and Beluga caviar. A small brasserie at the back also serves light meals.

14 **Angelo Lounge Bar**

72 Aleph Hotel, Via di San Basilio 15

Sipping a cocktail in a hotel bar has yet to become a truly established Roman habit, but the Aleph Hotel's Angelo Lounge Bar might change all that. Defined architecturally by a central luminescent white structure, it has red leather stools and plush sofas to tempt even the most Calvinist among us. Devilishly good Martinis are prepared by the resident barman. The Angelo bar is a small island amid the designer Adam Tihany's maximalist décor: it feels intimate yet sophisticated. The dark wood panelling and library add to the clubby atmosphere. Angelo's appeal lies in the fact that although hotel guests drift by it has yet to be fully discovered by the city's glitterati, so a drink here feels like a small, shared secret.

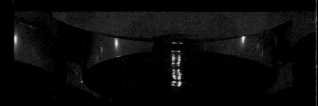

MUSICAL CHAIRS

92 **La Palma**

11 Via Giuseppe Mirri 35

Slightly off the beaten track, La Palma can be reached via a short taxi drive from the area of San Lorenzo. Over the past few years this club has become the address for jazz aficionados, offering a star-studded programme that can rival those of the more established venues in the centre of town. But there is also funk, African, Cuban and ethnic music. In the summer, the extensive grounds are decked with tents, an outdoor restaurant, bars and a concert area. The vibe is down to earth and relaxed, with enthusiastic crowds cheering their favourite artist. In the winter, concerts take place inside the space carved out from a disused warehouse, and there are disco nights. A good place to spot up-and-coming local and international talents.

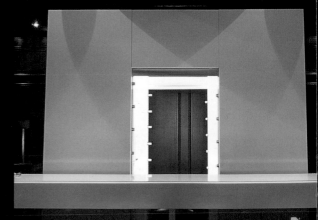

46 La Maison
46 Vicolo dei Granari 4

Opulently decorated with chandeliers and sofas, La Maison attracts a dressy crowd and the overspill from nearby Bloom (p. 156) at closing times. Guest DJs take to the decks on Tuesdays, while on Sundays there is a glitzy, gay-themed night. Owned by the same nightlife impresarios that run Le Bain (p. 77), La Maison is part of a new breed of design-conscious venues. Like many Roman bars, La Maison closes during summer to open an outdoor outpost. From June to September, this den of libertine excess relocates to the Palazzo dei Congressi in EUR, where the roof terrace offers uninterrupted views over the city's south side. The décor is sleekly minimal, with white plastic retro chairs, cubic structures and cushions in the lounge area. A blue neon light show follows the crowds of the dance floor. High octane indigenous glamour and a fun night out is guaranteed.

shop

As the home of Italian haute couture, Rome has long been associated with fashion. Legendary designers Valentino, Capucci, Fendi and Fontana all started here before acquiring international fame. The feel for old-world glamour is still intact in the ateliers that line the streets around Piazza di Spagna, and many boutiques take pride in providing high-quality tailoring. There is also a breed of independent designers who combine craftsmanship with a funkier, more individual sense of style. And thankfully, the international chains have yet to uproot the city's wealth of artisan shops, antique bookshops and traditional herbalists.

46 Ilaria Miani
17 Via del Monserrato 35

Even if you don't own a rambling Tuscan country home, you can bask in some of the style that Ilaria Miani – veteran restorer of farmhouses – has injected into her elegant line of furnishings. 'Prudently modern' items include striped lampshades in all sizes, wooden coffee tables and shelves, outdoor furniture and even four-poster beds. All the pieces are handmade and fold flat for easy transport. And if it's just inspiration you are searching for, look no further than the myriad of international publications scattered around the shop featuring some of Miani's interior-design projects. For those interested in smaller purchases, Ilaria Miani has her own range of deliciously scented candles and perfumes, precious frames and coloured glassware.

HOUSE OF BRANDS
14 Degli Effetti
9 Piazza Capranica 75, 79 & 93

Italian celebrities and well-heeled fashionistas pop in to check on the latest arrivals at Degli Effetti, a temple to retail therapy with a tendency for quirky, individualistic pieces. Massimo Degli Effetti has been a pioneering retailer in Rome – he was one of the first in the 1980s to bring labels such as Prada, Jean-Paul Gaultier and Yohji Yamamoto under one roof for discerning male customers. A few years later he extended his concept to womenswear, always maintaining the vision of a small boutique where personalized service and knowledge of international fashion trends reign supreme. His boutiques in Piazza Capranica are still considered essential stops on the Saturday shopping route, with dedicated customers welcomed as old friends by the staff. The stores offer a clean, minimalist aesthetic with cleverly inventive window installations.

Bomba abbigliamento

Via dell'Oca 39

Sweet, pretty things can be found at Bomba, the shop that is in every Roman woman's little address book. Cristina's designs effortlessly combine understatement with a good splash of colour; her long linen dresses, the fine cotton T-shirts, vests and long-sleeve shirts are simple, pared-down creations that are wardrobe staples. Precious cashmere children's dresses by Ang e un Bebe and beaded bags hang on walls as installations, while a specific area is devoted to small designers who Cristina scours Italy for,

among them shoes by Henry Beguelin, jewelry by Donatella Pellini and Mother Superior T-shirts by Bettina Pontiggia, each of which bears the name of a celebrity, writer or filmmaker, like Pier Paolo Pasolini and Robin Hood. The menswear section is a kaleidoscopic display of ties, some even designed by architects Scarpa and Lapadula. Suits and dresses can be made to order in the upstairs workshop. A recent addition is the small gallery-cum-tearoom that provides an exhibition space for emerging Roman artists as well as the occasional catwalk show.

46 **L'una e L'altra**

32 Via del Governo Vecchio 105

Bibi and Luigi D'Alessio spearheaded a Roman love affair with deconstructed fashion when they opened L'una e L'altra in the 1980s. Initially devoted to Antwerp's designers, they later widened the range to include garments by Jean-Paul Gaultier and Issey Miyake. High-calibre Roman haute couture is also sold, including items by tailor Faliero Sarli. However, the shop's main selling point is having the exclusive franchise for Dries Van Noten. The boutique provides attentive customized service for its glamorous clientele: peering through the windows it is often possible to spot an Italian actress choosing an outfit for an award ceremony. Theatrical window displays lure passersby, and Bibi and Luigi's private collection of Ettore Sottsass's Memphis ceramic and glass vases is regularly updated to decorate the shelving units.

VINO VERITY
14 **Trimani**

79 Via Goito 20

Oenophiles will delight in finding Trimani, a slightly off-the-beaten-track wine emporium selling more than 5200 labels from around the world, as well as an excellent grappa and liqueur selection. Marco Trimani's family has been involved in the wine trade since 1821 when they owned a wine shop in central Via del Panico. They moved to the residential street of Via Goito near the Esquilino hill in 1876 just as the area was becoming fashionable with the Roman middle classes. Today, the 400-square-metre-space houses a shop, wine cellars and an upstairs wine bar. The most intriguing feature at Trimani is the bulk wine dispenser, a large block of Carrara marble sculpted as a fountain. Carved with bunches of grapes, it contains a water inlet connected to the Felice aqueduct that provided fresh-flowing water used to keep the wines cool. The wines used to be housed in urns and the brass plates show how much they cost in the 1920s: 5 Lire for the white and 4 Lire for the red.

Spare a thought for today's parents overwhelmed by plastic toys and make a detour for Città del Sole. Inside are beautifully crafted wooden toys – tricycles, fire engines, rocking horses – largely of Scandinavian manufacture. Their rotating night lights, with a farmhouse or a *Petit Prince* theme, are bestsellers despite the hefty price tag. Older kids are also catered for, with a wide selection of board games, puzzles and building kits. A small section is devoted to toys for adults, a wildly diverse assortment that ranges from new-age crystals to computer chessboards and compasses. Illustrated books by designers Bruno Munari and Enzo Mari are always popular, but check out the city maps and guides devised for children. Every present gets wrapped in the shop's signature paper, a rose and yellow tinted leitmotif that will make you popular at any birthday party.

This stunningly designed interiors shop – all concrete floors, flights of stairs and recessed backlit rooms – can be visited almost as an idealized route into the perfect home, where the steel-framed beds are made up with starched linen sheets and the atmosphere is calm and uncluttered. Magazzini Associati is the exclusive agent for Rome's De Padova line; it also stocks wicker creations by Gervasoni and lights by FontanaArte. Smaller items include Hickman Tools kitchenware designed by Antonio Citterio and Boffi's bathroom fittings as well as a delectable linen nightwear and daywear collection. Most items will be too big to fit into a suitcase, but the shop deserves a visit if only for its uncompromising devotion to contemporary minimalist living.

46 Spazio Sette

3 Via dei Barbieri 7

Housed in a converted three-floor frescoed 17th-century palazzo, Spazio Sette manages to escape a reputation for being 'just another design emporium' with a wondrous selection of items small and large. Although it does sell the ubiquitous design names (Marimekko, Driade and Venini) – and many pieces are so big that they would have to be shipped back home – it also has a wide choice of smaller Italian names not found elsewhere that work well as original gifts. Handmade glass tableware from La Compagnia del Tabacco, carved wood table mats by Legnomagica, ceramic serving tables by Rina Menardi and ethnic-inspired, chunky necklaces designed by Angela Caputi are among its wares.

DE GUSTIBUS

14 Gusto's Emporio Libreria

38 Piazza Augusto Imperatore 9

Located between the Ara Pacis and the Mausoleum of Augustus is the Gusto eaterie (p. 144), a stylish and popular establishment, which is both a restaurant (Gusto), a wine bar and trattoria (Osteria della Frezza). Gusto's reputation as a gastronomic empire could not be fully justified without its definitive kitchen shop. Decked out in steel and blonde wood, the shop is a series of narrow rooms packed to the rafters with kitchen utensils and gadgets, wicker baskets and starched linens. Browse for books on Italian regional cooking, like Ada Boni's seminal volume on Roman cuisine as well as international gourmet finds such as El Bulli's chef Adrian Ferra's glossy, limited edition coffee table cookbooks. Snap up a precious crystal wine decanter or a pretty china boat-shaped olive holder. Ask the courteous and well-informed staff to advise you on a bottle from the well-stocked wine section at the back.

TOOLS FOR COOKS

14 C.U.C.I.N.A

52 Via Mario de' Fiori 65

A more utilitarian kitchen shop than Gusto's, C.U.C.I.N.A caters for all those savvy cooks who take delight in ceramic knives and Alessi cafetières. The original flagship store was located in Via del Babuino, and for years was a mecca for discerning shoppers who would flock here to snap up the latest aluminium salad spinner. There are no big brands here, rather a functional selection of kitchenware to serve all purposes. Relocated to Via Mario de' Fiori (and with two other shops outside the city centre), C.U.C.I.N.A is a minimally decorated four-room space. Funky flatpack laundry bags that open up in the shape of a washing machine, elegant linen aprons and tea-towels, chunky glassware and white china plates are among the shop's finds.

14 Dal Cò

50 Via Vittoria 65

Imelda Marcos eat your heart out should be Dal Cò's promotional tag as this tiny shop in a hidden street just off crowded Via del Corso is a temple to shoe fetishism. Each pair is lovingly handmade: a gentleman traces your feet, you return three days later for a fitting and a week after that you are presented with a unique pair of made-to-measure shoes. For those feeling extravagant there is even the possibility of having a handbag made to match. Most of Dal Cò's shoes are low key and pretty conservative in style, featuring ankle straps, suede and flannels and comfortable pumps. But their evening collection is far more adventurous, with heels decorated with tiny beads, sandals with marabou feathers and pretty fabric flowers. Audrey Hepburn and Ava Gardner loved the place and it is easy to see why.

14 Battistoni

59 Via Condotti 60–61a

Those who remember Jude Law in *The Talented Mr Ripley* will recognize the name of Battistoni, whom he visits for a bespoke suit during his visit to Rome. Well placed in a beautiful courtyard off chic shopping strip Via Condotti, Battistoni has been 'the Italian tailor' for decades, known for his classic and elegant style. An endless list of movie stars, Italian TV presenters and journalists shop here and his name constantly appears in TV programmes and film credits. Inside the shop it is as if time has stood still, with flawless service delivered by elegant shop assistants in the teak-clad women's boutique and distinguished gentlemen in the historic men's department. Rare artworks hang on the walls and antique furniture pieces rub shoulders with the clothes. Battistoni's forte is custom-made suits for women and men, but it also sells ready-to-wear labels. Only the best silks, cashmeres and linens are used and there is a very efficient alteration service always on hand.

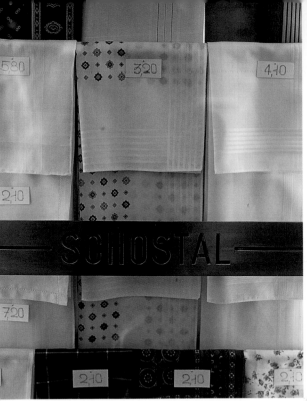

LEATHER LEGEND

14

5
Federico Polidori

Via di Piè di Marmo 7–8

Federico Polidori is what Rome does best, a craft workshop that creates high quality leather bags and accessories. Polidori designs each bag and briefcase with the client and then sews it by hand. His tiny shop alongside Via di Piè di Marmo is a firm favourite among the Roman aristocracy, who stop by to commission monogrammed travelling bags or even a bespoke rifle bag for their hunting trips. Inside, the sheets of cowhide leather are hung waiting to be expertly treated, hand cut and hand stitched. All around are selected decorative items that recall his craft: battered vintage travelling suitcases, old tins of leather wax and oils, tools and brushes. Federico Polidori is an unassuming, charming man, his hands working the leathers swiftly into beautiful, precious shapes.

SUPERIOR SOCKS

14

58
Schostal

Via del Corso 158

Leave the traffic noise of shopping route Via del Corso for a moment and step back in time by entering Schostal. Gentlemen come here to stock up on wardrobe essentials, such as pocket handkerchiefs and pyjamas. But it's the socks that really make Schostal such a find – super soft and light, they come in cotton, silk, plain wool and cashmere. Inside, the quaint décor is pretty much like it was when it opened in 1870. Dark wood cabinets, chests of drawers and shelves are laden with men's shirts, bows and scarves. There is also a women's section, offering traditionally cut, understated nightgowns and underwear. Endearingly, all the price tags are handwritten, with a sprawly calligraphy that fits well with the ambience. The flawless service, despite of the occasional long queue, has customers coming back for more.

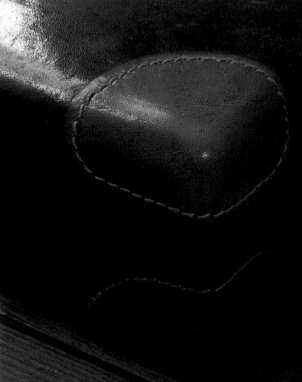

Global brand Bulgari started small when Sotirio Bulgari arrived from Greece in 1895 and set up shop in Via Sistina. The Via Condotti shop was opened in 1905 and today features palatial architecture that reflects the jeweler's opulent style. Old coins set in gold, cabochon-cut precious stones and lots of glittering metals are the trademark of this iconic name, which with its collections *Parentesi*, *Tubogas* and *Spiga* became a firm favourite of the fashionable jet set in the 1960s. Today the business is still family run, with Giorgio and Paolo Bulgari at the helm and their nephew Francesco Trapani steering it towards a design-led direction. After expanding into watches and perfumes, Bulgari recently forayed into the world of boutique hotels, with one designed by Citterio in Milan and two more in the pipeline.

The doyennes of Roman haute couture, Sorelle Fontana, shot to international fame in 1949 when they designed Linda Christian's dress for her opulent and much publicized wedding to Tyrone Power in the church of Santa Francesca Romana. Hollywood and America's wealthy classes soon followed and the designers became synonymous with fairytale wedding dresses. Years earlier, the three sisters, Zoe, Micol and Giovanna, had left their tiny hometown of Traversetolo, near Parma, to try their luck in a larger city. Unable to decide between Milan and Rome, they agreed to take the first train that appeared. A train heading to Rome proved to be a fruitful decision. Today their boutique still retains the charm of a timeless atelier where sublime craftsmanship is employed to create extravagant one-offs. The label's current designer, Marco Coretti, creates dreamy pink chiffon evening gowns, funky crocodile leather jackets and diamante stilettos for modern day princesses.

For years the designer behind Costume National was a mystery as the fashion house's philosophy was that the clothes should do the talking. Ennio Capasa took the company's name from an antique book on French uniforms, and in 1987 proceeded to create a label that champions clean and chic minimalism. His designs for men and women never scream but cleverly wrap the silhouette with grace and a dash of humour. Capasa trained as an architect and designed this boutique in Rome as well as his other outlet in Milan. Strategically located in Via del Babuino, Costume National is a long, clean and sleek box lit by halogen lights. Neat rows of black coats hang next to turquoise trouser suits, while the exquisitely crafted leather shoes lined up on Perspex display units allow no distraction for the faithful customers who flock as soon as the new stock hits the shop.

If you don't know it, you will probably miss it, even though its location is bang in the centre of pretty Piazza della Rotonda in front of the Pantheon. It is listed as a historic shop, and rightly so. Founded in 1784, and still run by the same family, Giorgi e Febbi is a treasure trove of beautiful fabrics, printed using ancient techniques and manufactured in a workshop in the countryside outside Rome that has been and owned by the family for centuries. The shop has two floors crammed with Florentine-style flower and paisley patterns, silks and brocades, alongside fringed ribbons, braided cords and tassels. You can even bring in your own favourite fabric and have it reproduced by the local craftsmen. A truly precious find for those looking to decorate a home in an original style.

Judging from the photographs that line the shop's walls, everybody – from Elizabeth Taylor to George Clooney – seems to have bought a pair of hand-stitched gloves from Sermoneta. But regardless of the star kudos that this shop, which was established in 1967, carries, there is little doubt about the quality of its product. Sixty colours, six sizes – including extra small and extra large – kid, boar, ostrich and crocodile leathers, cashmere or wool, with stitching or with silk lining, each pair is expertly and lovingly produced in the Sermoneta factory. The Spanish Steps flagship store has recently been given a makeover, and the gleaming new display units and shopfitting details are an anticipation of the new look that will soon roll out in Madrid and London (there are shops in Milan, and over 55 franchises around the world). Giorgio Sermoneta and his family run their shop with a warm, personal touch, dispensing words of advice – where to eat and what to see – to any discerning customer that pops by.

64 Scala Quattordici

6 Via della Scala 14

Letterio Attanasio and Giuseppe Michelini are the talents behind Scala Quattordici, a semi-hidden womenswear boutique in the heart of Trastevere. Employing a multicoloured array of silks, cottons and linens from fashion labels like Ungaro and Valentino, they create bespoke, limited edition pieces that are loved by Rome's most fashionable customers. The attraction of Scala Quattordici is undoubtedly its attentive and personalized service – no rush seems to be the owners' mantra with plenty of time for fittings, choosing favourite styles and models and even to have a leisurely chat on the sofas. The look is pretty and feminine rather than cutting edge, and suits those looking for an outfit for a romantic or special occasion. Next door is the tailoring workshop, with its mannequins and piles of materials waiting to be rustled up into memorable creations.

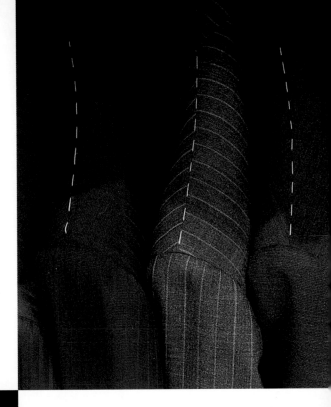

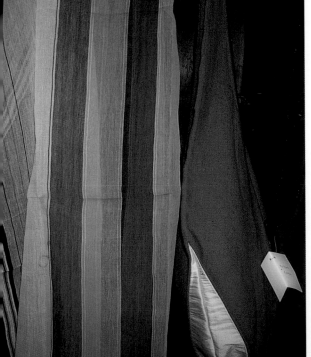

WELL SUITED

14 Davide Cenci

25 Via di Campo Marzio 1–7

Parliamentarians from nearby Montecitorio and Italian professionals with a passion for the 'gentleman' style are among Davide Cenci's most faithful customers. Founded in 1921, the boutique combines old-fashioned service (made-to-measure suits from the finest English flannels, home deliveries and shop assistants who know their customer's first name) with a wide range of Italian and international brands, such as Davide Cenci's own, Burberry, Ermenegildo Zegna and Ralph Lauren. This Roman institution now has another shop in Milan and one in New York, but only here you will catch *Signor* Cenci himself exchanging pleasantries with clients. The décor reflects the timeless elegance of the place – vast marble flooring, wood panelling in the tailoring sections and a grand staircase leading upstairs to where womenswear labels such as Pucci and Alberta Ferretti as well as accessories like ties, bags and hats are sold.

A TAD TRENDY

14 **TAD**

43 Via del Babuino 155a

Rome's very personal spin on a concept store, TAD stands for *tendenze e antiche debolezze*, meaning trends and old weaknesses. Indulge in this large retail heaven, designed to offer the most covetable creations by Alessandro Dell'Acqua, Alexander McQueen, Alberto Biani and Balenciaga, just a few of the labels on display. There is Far-Eastern inspired homeware by Marina Coffa and teak, mahogany and wicker furniture. Foreign magazines, art books and a selection of trip-hop, soul, latin, house, garage and lounge compilations grace the shelves. There is also a NuYorica shoe-shop concession (p. 52), a flower shop and a small hairdresser's. Exhausted shoppers can stop for a *macchiato* or green tea at the TAD Café, which has a refreshing outdoor courtyard space with seating by Philippe Starck and lighting by Ross Lovegrove. Lunch is also popular, with its Asian–Mediterranean fusion cuisine supervised by chef Anthony Genovese.

MODERN DAY ICONS
14 **Fendi**
62 Via Borgognona 36–40

Who hasn't ever desired a Baguette bag to tuck neatly under the arm? The Fendi sisters have been crafting fashion, accessories and furs in Rome since 1925, although it was third generation Silvia Venturini, Fendi's Creative Director, who put the label on the global map with this funky handbag, now a status symbol for the fashion world. Deceptively simple – a comfortable handbag with a short shoulder strap – the Baguette has become a cult object. Once a modest fur and leather goods store begun by Eduardo and Adele Fendi, Fendi developed thanks to the savvy management and creative flair of their daughters. The Via Borgognona store was opened by Paola, Anna, Franca, Carla and Alda Fendi in 1964, and a new addition is a dramatic-looking shop in Largo Goldoni. Karl Lagerfeld was brought in as a collaborator in 1965; it was he who designed the iconic double-F logo. Today Fendi is owned by Prada and Bernard Arnault, although the family retains the management. The style remains unashamedly luxurious and extremely collectable.

VERY VALENTINO
14 **Valentino**
55 Via Bocca di Leone 15. Via Condotti 13, Via del Babuino 6

From Sophia Loren to Julia Roberts, many stars have fallen for the talents of designer Valentino Garavani. Precious fabrics, exquisite craftsmanship and an unashamed passion for the colour red (now known as Valentino red) are among his trademarks. Valentino started his career with the shop in Via Condotti and then with an atelier in Via Gregoriana, the road favoured by Roman haute-couture fashion designers such as Roberto Capucci, Pino Lancetti and Fausto Sarli. Fast forward a couple of years and his headquarters are in Palazzo Mignanelli, a grandiose palace close to the Spanish Steps, from where he runs his global fashion empire and occasionally throws memorable parties for the jet set. The Via Condotti flagship still maintains its allure – the sleek display systems do not overwhelm the luxurious gowns and killer heels. There is also a men's store on Via Bocca di Leone, and a younger line, Valentino Roma, on Via del Babuino.

retreat

With so many places to visit within an hour's drive of the city, it is not surprising that a day trip out of Rome has been a tradition since ancient Roman times. The Tyrrhenian coast south of the city is dotted with resorts, from the family oriented to those that are wilder and more exclusive. North of the city, the region opens up to volcanic lakes, warm water springs and rows of vineyards. Those looking for culture can find archaeological remains, Renaissance villas and medieval towns, while a trip to the island of Ponza provides the perfect escapist weekend.

Ponza: Mediterranean Hideway

- Frontone Beach
- Orestorante
- Grand Hotel Santa Domitilla

Arriving by sea you are struck by the languid beauty of Ponza. Surprisingly, this tiny, rugged island off the Lazio coastline used to be a place of exile for Fascist dissidents. More recently, Ponza has become a playground for the fashionable and wealthy of Rome, who appreciate its wild charm, crystal-clear blue waters and stunning volcanic cliffs. A 90-minute hydrofoil journey from nearby Anzio means that the six kilometre-long island fills up during the peak holiday season (July and August) with weekenders escaping the city's sweltering heat. The main sandy beach of Frontone – which can be reached via local boats departing every ten minutes from the port – attracts a mix of young families and a more hedonistic party crowd who enjoy the beach-bar DJs' soundtrack while sunbathing. At about six o'clock the music is cranked up, the sign for bathers to head to the open-air bar to dance the night away. Later in the evening, stylish sun-worshippers slip into their eveningwear and join the affluent yacht crowd for a meal at Orestorante, one of Lazio's most highly rated establishments, stunningly located on a three-tiered terrace overlooking the harbour. Tagliatelle with almonds, cod roe and lemon zest and sea bass with black olives and fennel are among the delicacies that chef and owner Oreste rustles up.

Discerning travellers tend to arrive in Ponza slightly out of season, renting the pastel-hued houses or fishermen's rooms from the various letting agencies on the island. Although lodgings are abundant in Ponza, the Grand Hotel Santa Domitilla is a cut above your average family *pensione*. Owned by the family who also run the Gennarino a Mare restaurant on the seafront, the Santa Domitilla's greatest attraction is its landscaped swimming pool, dug into old caves traditionally used by the locals as cellars. The hotel itself has white plaster exteriors and vivid blue hand-painted tiles, driftwood used as decoration throughout and a Mediterranean garden filled with prickly pear plants, bougainvillea, lemon and fig trees.

Frascati: Hedonistic Villa Trail

- Villa Grazioli
- Cacciani

When the Rome–Frascati railway line was built in 1865, the day trip from Rome to taste the Frascati wines became so popular that the last train back to the city was nicknamed the 'drunk' train. But a day trip to nearby Frascati (it's a 30-minute drive from the city) has long been an institution for Romans who would pack a picnic hamper and stop at the numerous *fraschette* (outdoor wine bars) to sample the honey-scented nectar. After a period in the doldrums, the wines of Frascati are today enjoying a well-deserved revival, with top producers Castel de Paolis and Paola di Mauro churning out more than decent bottles. The area is also well known for the beautiful Tuscolo villas – a legacy of the 16th century, when the Roman aristocratic families of Aldobrandini, Lancellotti, Falconieri, Mondragone, Parisi, Muti, Grazioli and Torlonia built grandiose palaces as a symbol of their power. You can follow the well-trodden path along these rolling hills, admiring stunning villas like the Aldobrandini, whose landscaped gardens are erratically open to the public, and enjoy a stay in one that has been converted into a hotel, such as the grandiose Villa Grazioli. Set in a 15,000-square-metre garden on the edge of a ridge, the 16th-century villa boasts amazing views over Rome. The one time home of Cardinal Carafa features faded frescoes, Italian antiques, trompe l'oeils and a small chapel consecrated to St John the Baptist. Pale blues, dusty pinks and golden hues on the walls complement the ancient terracotta-tiled floors and marble inserts, while the bedrooms are more sombre in their modern décor, but comfortable. Back in town, a bottle of Frascati wine should be ordered at Cacciani, a friendly and buzzing establishment serving innovati Italian cuisine and a few of the area's classics, including squid bruschetta melted provolone cheese. The restaurant is highly rated among fo regulars, so book ahead.

ANCIENT VILLAS AND PAST MEMORIES

Villa Adriana and Villa d'Este: Roman Splendour, Baroque Excess

• Hotel Adriano
• Villa d'Este

A mere 20 kilometres from Rome is the town of Tivoli, built on the slopes of the Sabine hills, popular since ancient times with Roman aristocrats. The Emperor Hadrian built his villa here in the 2nd century AD as a testimony to his passion for architecture (much of the design was his own), Greek culture and beauty. The villa consisted of an imperial palace, baths, libraries and gardens full of sculptures and pools. Although many of the original mosaics and statues are now housed in museums around the world, remnants of the villa's rich decoration remain, with multicoloured inlaid marble floors and traces of wall painting. In the summer, open-air theatre performances and concerts are held among the spectacular ruins, the elegant architecture providing the perfect backdrop for serene contemplation. Just in front of the villa lies the small but charming Hotel Adriano. Writer Marguerite Yourcenar stayed here while writing her book, *Hadrian's Memories*, a fictionalized biography of Hadrian and a moving insight into the life and passions of this learned man. Lovingly run by the Cinelli family, the 19th-century red villa might have modest rooms, but it compensates for this with attentive service and attractive gardens. In the evening, those romantically inclined can enjoy the ivy clad, al fresco dining area, and be surprised by an excellent menu of homemade fettuccine with herbs, pecorino and pine nuts, or the adventurous dish of flowers and leaves fried in tempura batter.

If the serene beauty of Villa Adriana is too subdued, try the more excessive Villa d'Este, a riot of Baroque decoration, built during the late 16th century by Lucretia Borgia's son, Cardinal Ippolito d'Este. With its geometric patterns, 500 fountains and ancient and rare trees, this is one of the finest gardens in Italy. The humming fountains are music in themselves and provide an experience of sensual overload.

Sabaudia and Circeo: Architecture and Nature

- Complesso Punta Rossa
- Hotel Torre Paola
- Saporetti

Nowhere is the legacy of Fascist architecture more serene looking than in the seaside town of Sabaudia, founded in 1934 a mere hundred kilometres from Rome. According to Fascist propaganda, Sabaudia was built in 253 days by 6,000 men working day and night. Constructed as part of a scheme to regenerate the marshlands around the Agro Pontino area, today the town is a revered gem of Rationalist architecture, with public buildings such as the post office and the town hall set amid palm trees and purple bougainvillea.

Away from the utopian town is a spectacular stretch of sandy dunes and Mediterranean bush – the beach of Sabaudia. This is the domain of day-trippers from Rome as well as Italian movie stars who retreat into their semi- hidden beach houses and villas built (illegally) during the 1960s among the dunes. At the end of the beach lies Saporetti, the fashionable restaurant patronized by the media crowd who strike film deals over steaming *spaghetti alle vongole*. Just at its feet lies Monte Circeo, a national park since the 1960s, and next to which the Hotel Torre Paola is located, a 13th-century listed building recently restored into a stylish 15-room hotel. The hotel's grounds feature a church and a beautiful garden with tamarind trees, as well as overlooking the canal. From here it's a detour of about ten kilometres towards Punta Rossa, on the opposite side of Monte Circeo, where a super-exclusive hotel resort is located on the gently sloping cliffs. Built in the 1950s by the architect Michele Busiri Vici, Punta Rossa Hotel is a fascinating mix of vernacular period architecture and modern-day luxuries, such as a salt-water landscaped pool and a spa with thalasso therapy. Guests can either check in to the main hotel or take one of the wonderful whitewashed villas for a longer period.

contact

All telephone numbers are given for dialling locally: the country code for Italy is 39; the city code for Rome, which must be included even when calling locally, is 06. Calling from abroad, one dials (+39) plus the number given below. Telephone numbers in the Retreat section are given for dialling from Rome: if calling from abroad, dial the country code (+39) followed by the number given. The number in brackets by the name is the page number on which the entry appears.

Agata e Romeo [145]
Via Carlo Alberto 45
00185 Rome
T   06 44 66 115
F   06 44 65 842
E   ristorante@agataeromeo.it
W   www.agataeromeo.it

Akab [86]
Via di Monte Testaccio 69
00153 Rome
T/F 06 57 82 390
W   www.akabcave.com

Al Bric [143]
Via del Pellegrino 51–52
00186 Rome
T   06 68 79 533
E   info@albric.it
W   www.albric.it

Alberto Ciarla [140]
Piazza di San Cosimato 40
00153 Rome
T   06 58 18 668
F   06 58 84 377
E   alberto@albertociarla.com
W   www.albertociarla.com

Aleph Hotel [128]
Via di San Basilio 15
00187 Rome
T   06 42 29 01
F   06 42 29 0000
E   reservation@aleph.boscolo.com
W   www.boscolohotels.com

Alibi [89]
Via di Monte Testaccio 40–44
00153 Rome
T/F 06 57 43 448
E   info@alibionline.it

Alpheus [89]
Via del Commercio 36
00154 Rome
T   06 57 47 826
E   alpheus@libero.it
W   www.alpheus.it

L'Altro di Mastai [136]
Via Giovanni Giraud 53
00186 Rome
T   06 68 30 1296
F   06 68 61 303
E   restaurant@laltromastai.it
W   www.laltromastai.it

Angelo di Nepi [48]
Via dei Giubbonari 28
00186 Rome
T   06 68 93 006
E   info@angelodinepi.it
W   www.angelodinepi.it

Angelo Lounge Bar [158]
Aleph Hotel
Via di San Basilio 15
00187 Rome
T   06 42 29 01
F   06 42 29 0000
W   www.boscolohotels.com

Antica Cartotecnica [18]
Piazza dei Caprettari 61
00186 Rome
T   06 68 75 671
F   06 68 77 093
E   info@anticacartotecnica.it
W   www.anticacartotecnica.it

L'Antica Erboristeria [60]
Via di Torre Argentina 15
00186 Rome
T   06 68 79 493
W   www.anticaerboristeria
romana.it

Antico Arco [136]
Piazzale Aurelio 7
00152 Rome
T   06 58 15 274

Arancia Blu [94]
Via dei Latini 55, 65
00185 Rome
T   06 44 54 105

Arancio d'Oro [27]
Via di Monte d'Oro 17
00186 Rome
T   06 68 65 026

Arsenale [59]
Via del Governo Vecchio 64
00186 Rome
T   68 61 380

Atelier Monti [100]
Via Panisperna 42

00184 Rome
T   06 47 82 4314
F   06 47 88 5042
E   info@ateliermonti.it
W   www.ateliermonti.it

**Auditorium Parco
della Musica** [42]
Viale Pietro de Coubertin 30
00196 Rome
T/F 06 80 24 111
F   06 80 241 211
E   info@musicaperroma.it
W   www.musicaperroma.it

Augustarello [84]
Via Giovanni Branca 98
00153 Rome
T   06 57 46 585

Baba [146]
Via Casale di Tor di Quinto 1
00191 Rome
T   06 33 30 745
W   www.babaristorante.it

Le Bain [77]
Via delle Botteghe Oscure 33
00186 Rome
T   06 68 65 673
E   lebain@tiscali.it
W   www.lebain.it

Bar del Fico [155]
Piazza del Fico 24–25
00186 Rome
T   06 68 75 568

F   06 68 76 880
E   ilfico@ilfico.com
W   www.ilfico.com

Bar Farnese [48]
Piazza Farnese 106–107
00186 Rome
T   06 68 80 2125

Il Bar della Pace [151]
Via della Pace 4–7
00186 Rome
T   06 68 61 216

Bar San Calisto [157]
Piazza di San Calisto
00153 Rome
T   06 58 35 869

Bar Tartaruga [77]
Piazza Mattei
00186 Rome

Bar Vitti Centro [23]
Piazza di San Lorenzo in Lucina 33
00186 Rome
T   06 68 76 304

Bar Zest [99]
Via Filippo Turati 171
00185 Rome
T   06 44 48 41
F   06 44 34 1396
W   www.eshotel.it

Basilica di San Clemente [108]
Via di San Giovanni in Laterano
00184 Rome

Battistoni [168]
Via Condotti 60–61a
00187 Rome
T   06 69 76 111

Baullà [50]
Via dei Baullari 37
00186 Rome
T   06 68 67 670

Bibli [70]
Via dei Fienaroli 28
00153 Rome
T   06 58 14 534
W   www.bibli.it

Il Bicchiere di Mastai [151]
Via dei Banchi Nuovi 52
00186 Rome
T   06 68 19 2228

Bleve [74]
Via di Santa Maria del Pianto 9a–11
00186 Rome
T   06 68 65 970

Bloom [156]
Via Teatro Pace 30
00186 Rome
T   06 68 80 2029

Boccondivino [24]
Piazza in Campo Marzio, 6
00186 Rome
T   06 68 30 8626

E   info@boccondivino.it
W   www.boccondivino.it

Boccon Divino ristorante [56]
Vicolo del Pavone 2
00186 Rome
T   06 68 13 5051

Bomba abbigliamento [163]
Via dell'Oca 39
00186 Rome
T   06 32 03 020

Bonpoint [23]
Piazza di San Lorenzo in Lucina 25
00186 Rome
T   06 68 71 548

La Bottega del Cioccolato [100]
Via Leonina 82
00184 Rome
T   06 48 21 473

Bramante Cloister [60]
Vicolo del Arco della Pace 5
00186 Rome
T   06 68 80 9098

Bulgari [170]
Via Condotti 10
00187 Rome
T   06 69 62 61
F   06 67 83 419
W   www.bulgari.com

Bush [86]
Via Galvani 44
00153 Rome
T   06 57 28 8691

Café Café [110]
Via dei Santi Quattro Coronati 44
00184 Rome
T   06 70 08 743

Café De Oriente [86]
Via di Monte Testaccio 36
00153 Rome
T   06 57 45 019

Caffè Greco [153]
Via Condotti 86
00187 Rome
T   06 67 91 700

Caffè Latino [86]
Via di Monte Testaccio 96
00153 Rome
T   06 57 28 8556

Caffè Romano [154]
Hotel d'Inghilterra
Via Borgognona 4
00187 Rome
T   06 69.98 1500

Il Caffè di Sant'Eustachio [153]
Piazza di Sant'Eustachio 82
00186 Rome
T   06 68 80 20 48
W   www.santeustachioilcaffe.it

Caffè Tazza D'Oro [152]
Via degli Orfani 84
00186 Rome

T   06 67 89 792
F   06 67 98 131
E   info@tazzadorocoffeeshop.com
W   www.tazzadorocoffeeshop.com

Caffeteria Capitolina [77]
Piazza Caffarelli 4
00186 Rome
T   06 36 12 325

La Campana [142]
Vicolo della Campana 18
00186 Rome
T   06 68 67 820

Casa Bleve [152]
Via del Teatro Valle 48–49
00186 Rome
T   06 68 65 970
E   info@casableve.it
W   www.casableve.it

Casa Howard [122]
Via di Capo Le Case 18
00187 Rome
T   06 69 92 4555
F   06 67 94 644
E   info@casahoward.it
W   www.casahoward.com

Casina Valadier [41]
Villa Borghese
Piazza Bucarest
00187 Rome
T   06 69 92 2090
F   06 67 91 280
E   info@casinavaladier.it
W   www.casinarvaladier.it

Centrale Montemartini [89]
Collezioni dei Musei Capitolini
Via Ostiense 106
00154 Rome
T   06 57 48 030

Checchino dal 1887 [137]
Via di Monte Testaccio 30
00153 Rome
T   06 57 43 816
F   06 57 46 318
E   checchino_roma@tin.it
W   www.checchino-dal-1887.com

Cimitero Inglese [89]
Via Caio Cestio 6
00153 Rome
T   06 57 41 900
W   www.protestantcemetery.it

Città del Sole [165]
Via della Scrofa 65
00186 rome
T   06 68 80 3805
W   www.cittadelsole.it

Claudio Sano [96]
Largo degli Osci 67a
00185 Rome
T   06 44 69 284
E   info@claudiosano.it
W   www.claudiosano.it

Colline Emiliane [34]
Via degli Avignonesi 22

00187 Rome
T   06 48 17 538

**Confetteria Moriondo
e Gariglio** [17]
Via di Piè di Marmo 21–22
00186 Rome
T   06 69 90 856

Costume National [171]
Via del Babuino 106
00187 Rome
T   06 69 20 0686
F   06 67 85 829
W   www.costumenational.com

Crab [111]
Via Capo d'Africa 2
00184 Rome
T   06 77 20 3636

Crudo [154]
Via degli Specchi 6
00186 Rome
T   06 68 38 989

C.U.C.I.N.A [167]
Via Mario de' Fiori 65
00187 Rome
T   06 69 94 0819

Cul de Sac [138]
Piazza di Pasquino 73
00186 Rome
T   06 68 80 1094

Da Baffetto [59]
Via del Governo Vecchio 114
00186 Rome
T   06 68 61 617

Da Felice [86]
Via Mastro Giorgio 29
00153 Rome
T   06 57 46 800

Da Settimio all'Arancio [27]
Via dell'Arancio 50–52
00186 Rome
T   06 68 76 119

Dal Cò [168]
Via Vittoria 65
00187 Rome
T   06 67 86 536

Davide Cenci [173]
Via di Campo Marzio 1–7
00186 Rome
T   06 69 90 681
F   06 67 95 900
E   info@davidecenci.com
W   www.davidecenci.com

Degli Effetti [162]
Piazza Capranica 75, 79 &93
00186 Rome
T   06 68 13 4648
E   info@deglieffetti.com
W   www.deglieffetti.com

**Il desiderio preso
per la coda** [27]
Vicolo della Palomba 23

00186 Rome
T 06 68 30 75 22

Diego Percossi Papi [20]
Via di Sant'Eustachio 16
00186 Rome
T 06 68 80 1466

Ditirambo [50]
Piazza della Cancelleria 74–75
00186 Rome
T 06 68 71 626
W www.ristoranteditirambo.it

Il Dito e la Luna [95]
Via dei Sabelli 51
00185 Rome
T 06 49 40 726

Divinare [113]
Via Ostilia 4
00184 Rome
T 06 70 96 381

La Dolce Roma [73]
Via del Portico D'Ottavia 20b
00186 Rome
T 06 68 92 196

Domus Aurea [108]
Viale dell Domus Aurea
00184 Rome
T 06 39 74 9907/ 06 85 30 1758
Reservations are required.

Doney [39]
Via Vittorio Veneto 125
00187 Rome
T 06 47 08 2805

Dulce Vidoza [27]
Via dell'Orso 58
00186 Rome
T 06 68 93 007

Eleuteri [33]
Via Condotti 69
00187 Rome
T 06 67 83 119

L'Enoteca Antica [30]
Via della Croce 76b
00187 Rome
T 06 67 90 896
F 06 67 97 544

Enoteca Ferrara [139]
Piazza Trilussa 41
00153 Rome
T 06 58 333 920
F 06 58 03 769

Enoteca Il Piccolo [59]
Via del Governo Vecchio 74–75
00186 Rome
T 06 88 01 746

Ex Magazzini [89]
Via dei Magazzini Generali 8 bis
00154 Rome
T 06 57 58 040

Fabio Piccioni [103]
Via del Boschetto 148

00184 Rome
T 06 47 41 697

Fabio Salini [55]
Via di Monserrato 18
00186 Rome
T 06 68 30 11 72
F 06 68 13 45 67
E info@fabiosalini.it
W www.fabiosalini.it

Fausto Santini [33]
Via Frattina 120
00187 Rome
T 06 67 84 114

Federico Polidori [169]
Via di Piè di Marmo 7–8
00186 Rome
T 06 67 97 191

Fendi [175]
Via Borgognona 36–40
00187 Rome
T 06 69 66 661
W www.fendi.it

Ferrazza [99]
Via dei Volsci 59
00185 Rome
T 06 49 05 06
F 06 23 32 17 474

F.I.S.H – Fine International Seafood House [100]
Via dei Serpenti 16
00184 Rome
T 06 47 82 49 62
E info@f-i-s-h.it
W www.f-i-s-h.it

François Boutique [103]
Via del Boschetto 3
00184 Rome

Galleria Alberto Sordi [33]
Piazza Colonna 31–35
00187 Rome

Galleria Arte e Pensieri [108]
Via Ostilia 3a
00184 Rome
T 06 70 02 404
E artepensieriroma@libero.it

Galleria Borghese [41]
Piazzale del Museo Borghese 5
00197 Rome
T 06 84 13 979/06 32 810
W www.galleriaborghese.it

Galleria Doria Pamphilj [16]
Piazza del Collegio Romano 2
00186 Rome
T 06 67 97 323
F 06 67 80 939
E arti.rm@doriapamphilj.it
W www.doriapamphilj.it

Galleria Lorcan O'Neill [69]
Via degli Orti d'Alibert 1e
00165 Rome
T 06 68 89 29 80

Galleria Nazionale d'Arte Antica di Palazzo Barberini [34]
Via delle Quattro Fontane 13
00184 Rome
T 06 48 14 591
W www.galleriaborghese.it/
barberini/it

Galleria Pino Casagrande [95]
Via degli Ausoni 7a
00185 Rome
T/F 06 44 63 480

Galleria Sales [69]
Via San Francesco di Sales 16a
00165 Rome
T 06 68 80 6212
F 06 68 80 62 12
E sales@getnet.it

Le Gallinelle [103]
Via del Boschetto 76
00184 Rome
T 06 48 81 017
W www.legallinelle.it

Gente [30]
Via del Babuino 80–82
00187 Rome
T 06 32 07 671

Giggetto [73]
Via del Portico D'Ottavia 21a–22
00186 Rome
T 06 68 61 105
F 06 68 32 106
W www.giggettoalportico.com

Giolitti [24]
Via degli Uffici del Vicario 40
00186 Rome
T 06 69 91 243
F 06 69 94 1758
W www.giolitti.it

Giorgi e Febbi s.r.l. [172]
Piazza della Rotonda 61–62
00186 Rome
T 06 67 91 649

Il Goccetto [56]
Via dei Banchi Vecchi 14
00186 Rome
T 06 68 64 268

Gran Crowne Hotel Plaza Minerva [18]
Piazza della Minerva 69
00186 Rome
T 06 69 52 01
F 06 67 94 165
E minerve.res@hotel-invest.com
W www.grandhoteldelaminerve.it

Gusto Emporio Libreria [167]
Piazza Augusto Imperatore 9
00186 Rome
T 06 32 36 363
W www.gusto.it

Herzel [34]
Via di Propaganda 14
00187 Rome
T 06 67 95 114

Hostaria dell'Orso [139]
Via dei Soldati 25c
00186 Rome
T 06 68 30 1192
F 06 68 21 7063
E info@hostariadellorso.it
W www.hdo.it

Hosteria del Pesce [55]
Via di Monserrato 32
00186 Rome
T 06 68 65 617

Hotel Art [118]
Via Margutta 56
00187 Rome
T 06 32 87 11
F 06 36 00 3995
E info@hotelart.it
W www.hotelart.it

Hotel Capo d'Africa [132]
Via Capo d'Africa 54
00184 Rome
T 06 77 28 01
F 06 77 28 08 01
E info@hotelcapodafrica.com
W www.hotelcapodafrica.com

Ilaria Miani [162]
Via di Monserrato 35
00186 Rome
T 06 68 33 160

Iron icon [53]
Via di Monserrato 35
00186 Rome
T/F 06 68 78 743

Joia Music Restaurant [86]
Via Galvani 20–22
00153 Rome
T 06 57 40 802
W www.joiacafe.it

Josephine de Huertas [59]
Via del Governo Vecchio 68
00186 Rome
T 06 68 76 586
E info@josephinedehuertas.com
W www.josephinedehuertas.com

The Keats–Shelley House [33]
Piazza di Spagna 26
00187 Rome
T 06 67 84 235
F 06 67 84 167
E info@keats-shelley-house.org
W www.keats-shelley-house.org

Ketumbar [86]
Via Galvani 24
00153 Rome
T/F 06 57 30 5338

Laura Urbinati [56]
Via dei Banchi Vecchi 50a
00186 Rome
T/F 06 68 13 6478
W www.lauraurbinati.com

Lavori Artigianali Femminili [34]
Via di Capo le Case 6

00187 Rome
T 06 67 92 992

Letico [86]
Via Galvani 64
00153 Rome
T 06 57 25 0539

La Libreria del Viaggiatore [51]
Via del Pellegrino 78
00186 Rome
T/F 06 68 80 1048

Loco [52]
Via dei Baullari 22
00186 Rome
T 06 68 80 8216

Macro [41]
Via Reggio Emilia 54
00198 Rome
T 06 67 10 70400
F 06 85 54 090
W www.macro.roma.museum

Macro al Mattatoio [89]
Piazza Orazio Giustiniani 4
00153 Rome
T 06 67 10 70400
W www.macro.roma.museum

Magazzini Associati [165]
Corso del Rinascimento
00186 Rome
T 06 68 13 5179
F 06 68 13 5182

La Maison [159]
Le terrazze summer Palazzo
dei Congressi
Vicolo dei Granari 4
00186 Rome
T 06 68 33 312

Margutta Vegetariano [138]
Via Margutta 118
00187 Rome
T 06 32 65 0577

Maria Teresa Gaudenzi [103]
Via del Boschetto 1b
00184 Rome
T 06 47 44 679
E 06 1900@1900.it
W www.1900.it

**Mario Squatriti
Restauri Artistici** [28]
Via di Ripetta 29
00186 Rome
T 06 36 10 232

Maurizio Grossi [29]
Via Margutta 109
00187 Rome
T/F 06 36 00 1935
E maurizio.grossi@fastwebnet.it
W www.mauriziogrossi.com

MAXXI [41]
Via Guido Reni 10
00196 Rome
T 06 32 02 438
F 06 32 23 931
W www.maxximuseo.org

Mel Giannino Stoppani [16]
Piazza dei Santissimi
Apostoli 59–65
00187 Rome
T 06 69 94 10 45
F 06 67 97 296
W www.melgianninostoppani.it

Mercato di Testaccio [86]
Piazza Testaccio
00153 Rome

Miss Sixty [29]
Via del Corso 510
00186 Rome
T 06 32 19 374
F 06 32 19 444
W www.misssixty.com

Moma [34]
Via di San Basilio 42–43
00187 Rome
T 06 42 01 17 98

Mondello Ottica [53]
Via del Pellegrino 97–98
00186 Rome
T 06 68 61 955
W www.mondeloottica.it

Monti Doc [99]
Via Giovanni Lanza 93
00184 Rome
T 06 48 72 696

Museo de Chirico [33]
Piazza di Spagna 31
00187 Rome
T/F 06 67 96 546
E fondazionedechirico@tiscali.it
W www.fondazionedechirico.it

Myriam B [96]
Piazza dei Sanniti 42
00185 Rome
T 06 33 85 901 526
Via dei Volsci 75
00185 Rome
T 06 44 36 1305
E info@myriamb.com
W www.myriamb.com

Le Naumachie [113]
Via Celimontana 7
00184 Rome
T 06 70 02 764

**Il Negozio Benedettino
della Badia Primaziale
di Sant'Anselmo** [84]
Piazza dei Cavalieri di Malta 5
00153 Rome

NuYorica [52]
Piazza Pollarola 36–37
00186 Rome
T 06 68 89 1243
E contact@nuyorica.it
W www.nuyorica.it

Obika [25]
Via dei Prefetti 26a
00186 Rome
T 06 68 32 630.

L'Olfattorio Bar à Parfums [28]
Via di Ripetta 34
00186 Rome
T/F 06 36 12 325
W www.olfattorio.it

Orto Botanico [66]
Largo Cristina di Svezia 24
00165 Rome
T 06 68 32 300/
06 68 30 0937

Osteria della Frezza [144]
Via della Frezza 16
00186 Rome
T 06 32 26 273
W www.gusto.it

**Palazzetto at the
International Wine
Academy** [120]
Vicolo del Bottino 8
00187 Rome
T 06 69 90 878
F 06 67 91 385
E info@wineacademyroma.com
W www.wineacademyroma.com

Palazzo Altemps [60]
Piazza Sant'Apollinare 44
00186 Rome
T 06 68 33 759

**Palazzo del Freddo di
Giovanni Fassi** [96]
Via Principe Eugenio 65–67
00185 Rome
T 06 44 64 740

Palazzo Spada [48]
Piazza Capo di Ferro 13
00186 Roma
T 06 68 74 893
W www.galleriaborghese.it

La Palma [158]
Via Giuseppe Mirri 35
00159 Rome
T 06 43 59 90 29
E info@lapalmaclub.it
W www.lapalmaclub.it

Panella [99]
Via Merulana 54–55
00185 Rome
T 06 48 72 344

Pantheon [18]
Piazza della Rotonda
00186 Rome
T 06 68 30 0230

Papagiò [110]
Via Capo d'Africa 26
00184 Rome
T 06 77 26 2953

Passamanerie Crocianelli [27]
Via dei Prefetti 37–40
00186 Rome
T 06 68 73 592

Pastore & Tjäder [103]
Via della Madonna dei Monti 62a

00184 Rome
T 06 47 82 2332

Al Piccolo Arancio [27]
Vicolo Scanderberg 112
00187 Rome
T 06 67 86 139

Pierluigi [55]
Piazza dei Ricci 144
00186 Rome
T 06 68 61 302/
06 68 68 717
F 06 68 80 78 79
W www.pierluigi.it

Pommidoro [96]
Piazza dei Sanniti 44
00185 Rome
T 06 44 52 692

Pontificia Erboristeria [23]
Via del Pozzo delle Cornacchie 26
00186 Rome
T 06 68 61 201

Porta Portese [70]
Viale di Trastevere
00153 Rome

**Priorato dei Cavalieri
di Malta** [83]
Piazza dei Cavalieri di Malta 4
00153 Rome
T 06 57 79 193
W www.orderofmalta.org

Profumeria Materozzoli [23]
Piazza di San Lorenzo In Lucina 5
00186 Rome
T 06 68 89 2686

Radisson SAS [130]
Via Filippo Turati 171
00185 Rome
T 06 44 48 41
F 06 44 34 13 96
E info.roma@radissonsas.com
W www.radissonsas.com

Reef [27]
Piazza Augusto Imperatore 42–48
00186 Rome
T 06 66 83 01430
F 06 66 82 17532
E info@ristorantereef.it
W www.ristorantereef.it

Relais Banchi Vecchi [124]
Via dei Banchi Vecchi 115
00186 Rome
T 06 68 64 821
E info@banchivecchi115.com
W www.banchivecchi115.com

Riccioli Cafe [155]
Piazza delle Coppelle 10a
00186 Rome
T 06 68 21 0313

Ripa Hotel [126]
Via degli Orti di Trastevere 1
00153 Rome

T 06 58 611
F 06 58 14 550
W www.ripahotel.com

Ristorante il Pompiere [74]
Via di Santa Maria dei Calderari 38
00186 Rome
T 06 68 68 377

Ristorante Vecchia Roma [73]
Piazza di Campitelli 12
00186 Rome
T 06 68 64 604
W www.ristorantevecchiaroma.com

Roma Roma Roma [70]
Via dell'Arco dei Tolomei 2
00153 Rome
T 06 58 81 761

Roscioli [140]
Via dei Giubbonari 21–22a
00186 Rome
T 06 68 75 287
E info@rosciolifinefood.com
W www.rosciolifinefood.com

La Rosetta [142]
Via della Rosetta 8
00186 Rome
T 06 68 61 002
F 06 68 21 5116
E info@larosetta.com
W www.larosetta.com

**Il Roseto Comunale
di Roma** [82]
Clivio dei Pubblici
00153 Rome
T 06 57 46 810

Saint Regis Grand Hotel [36]
Via Vittorio Emanuele Orlando 3
00185 Rome
T 06 70 91
F 06 47 47 307
E stregisgrandrome@stregis.com
W www.stregis.com

**Sala degli Angeli,
Café de Paris** [38]
Via Vittorio Veneto 90
00187 Rome
T 06 48 85 284

San Daniele [74]
Piazza Mattei 16
00186 Rome
T 06 68 77 147

San Luigi dei Francesi [23]
Piazza di San Luigi dei Francesi 5
00186 Rome

San Marco [39]
Via Sardegna 38d
00187 Rome
T 06 42 824 893

San Teodoro [137]
Via dei Fienili 49–51
00186 Rome
T 06 67 80 933

Sant'Isidoro [37]
Via degli Artisti 41
00187 Rome
T 06 48 85 359

Sant'Andrea della Valle [21]
Piazza di Sant'Andrea della Valle
00186 Rome

Sant'Ivo alla Sapienza [21]
Corso del Rinascimento 40
00186 Rome

Santa Lucia [60]
Largo Febo 13
00186 Rome
T 06 68 80 2427
E info@santalucia-bartolo.com
W www.santalucia-bartolo.com

Santa Maria della Vittoria [37]
Via XX Settembre 17
00187 Rome

Santa Sabina [83]
Piazza Pietro d'Illiria
00153 Rome

Santi Quattro Coronati [108]
Via dei Santi Quattro Coronati
00184 Rome

Santo Stefano Rotondo [113]
Via di Santo Stefano Rotondo
00184 Rome

Scala Quattordici [173]
Via della Scala 14
00153 Rome
T 06 58 88 3580
F 06 58 34 5901

Schostal [169]
Via del Corso 158
00186 Rome
T 06 67 91 240

**Lo Scrittoio XXth
Century Design** [56]
Via dei Coronari 102–3
00186 Rome
T 06 68 75 536
F 06 97 84 0966

Scuderie del Quirinale [38]
Via XXIV Maggio 16
00187 Rome
T 06 39 96 7500
W www.scuderiequirinale.it

Sermoneta [172]
Piazza di Spagna 72a
00187 Rome
T 06 69 94 2110

Shaki Wine Bar [30]
Via Mario de' Fiori 29a
00187 Rome
T 06 67 91 694
W www.shakiroma.com

Il Simposio [150]
Piazza Cavour 16
00193 Rome
T 06 32 03 575

La Sinagoga [73]
Lungotevere dei Cenci
00186 Rome

Sisters [55]
Via dei Banchi Vecchi 143
00186 Rome
T 06 68 78 497

Sora Lella [143]
Via di Ponte Quattro Capi 16
Isola Tiberina
00186 Rome
T/F 06 68 61 601
W www.soralella.com

Sora Margherita [74]
Piazza Cinque Scole 30
00186 Rome
T 06 68 64 002

Sorelle Fontana [170]
Via della Fontanella di
Borghese 67–71
00186 Rome
T 06 68 13 5406
F 06 68 79 124

Spada [23]
Piazza di San Lorenzo in Lucina 20
00186 Rome
T 06 68 71 505

Spazio Sette [166]
Via dei Barbieri 7
00186 Rome
T 06 68 69 747
F 06 68 30 7139

**SBU – Strategic Business
Unit** [59]
Via di San Pantaleo 68–69
00186 Rome
T 06 68 80 2547

Suite at Ripa Hotel [70]
Via degli Orti di Trastevere 1
00153 Rome
T 06 58 611
F 06 58 14 550
E info@thesoundofsuite.com
W www.thesoundofsuite.com

Supperclub [141]
Via dei Nari 14
00173 Rome
T 06 68 80 7207
F 06 68 69 752
W www.supperclub.com

TAD [174]
Via del Babuino 155a
00187 Rome
T 06 32 69 5122

Le Tartarughe [17]
Via di Piè di Marmo 17, 33
00186 Rome
T 67 94 634
Via del Gesù 71a
00186 Rome

T/F 06 67 92 240
W www.susannalisoperle
     tartarughe.it

La Taverna degli Amici [77]
Piazza Margana 36–37
00186 Rome
T 06 69 92 0637
F 06 69 29 0826

La Taverna del Ghetto [73]
Via del Portico D'Ottavia 8
00186 Rome
T 06 68 80 9771
F 06 68 21 2309
W www.latavernadelghetto.com

Tazio [157]
Hotel Exedra
Piazza della Repubblica 47
00185 Rome
T 06 48 93 81
F 06 48 93 8000
E info@tazio.biz
W www.tazio.biz

Teatro di Documenti [89]
Via Nicola Zabaglia 42
00153 Rome
T 06 57 44 034
W www.teatrodidocumenti.it

Teatro Valle [20]
Via del Teatro Valle 21
00186 Rome
T 06 68 80 3794
W www.teatrovalle.it

**Tempi Moderni
1880–1980** [59]
Via del Governo Vecchio 108
00186 Rome
T 06 68 77 007

Tombolini [23]
Via della Maddalena 31–38
00186 Rome
T 06 69 20 0342
F 06 69 92 4608
W www.tombolini.it

Tram Tram [94]
Via dei Reti 44–46
00185 Rome
T 06 49 04 16

Trattoria [147]
Via del Pozzo delle Cornacchie 25
00186 Rome
T 06 68 30 1427
F 06 82 15 361
E info@ristorantetrattoria.it
W www.ristorantetrattoria.it

Trimani [164]
Via Goito 20
00185 Rome
T 06 44 69 661

L'una e l'altra [164]
Via del Governo Vecchio 105
00186 Rome
T 06 68 80 4995

Uno e Bino [147]
Via degli Equi 50
00185 Rome
T   06 44 60 702

Valentino [175]
Via Bocca di Leone 15
Via Condotti 13
00184 Rome
W   www.valentino.it

Valentino [restaurant] [100]
Via del Boschetto 37
00184 Rome
T   06 48 80 643

Valzani [69]
Via del Moro 37b
00153 Rome
T   06 58 03 792

Vestiti Usati Cinzia [59]
Via del Governo Vecchio 45
00186 Rome
T   06 68 61 791

Villa Celimontana [113]
Via della Navicella
00184 Rome
W   www.villacelimontanajazz.com

Villa Farnesina [66]
Via della Lungara 230
00165 Rome
T   06 68 02 7267
F   06 68 02 7345
E   farnesina@lincei.it

Villaggio Globale [86]
Via del Monte dei Cocci 22
00153 Rome
T   06 57 57 233

La Vineria Reggio [156]
Piazza Campo de' Fiori 15
00186 Rome
T   06 68 80 3268

Al Vino Al Vino [100]
Via dei Serpenti 19
00184 Rome
T   06 48 58 03

Vizi Capitali [69]
Vicolo della Renella 94
00153 Rome
T   06 58 18 840
E   vizicapitali@tiscali.it
W   www.vizicapitali.com

Volpetti [85]
Via Marmorata 47
00153 Rome
T   06 57 42 352
Via Alessandro Volta 8
00153 Rome
T   06 57 44 305
W   www.volpetti.com

Yien [23]
Via di Campo Marzio 33
00186 Rome
T   06 68 71 346

PONZA [178]

Hydrofoils to Ponza leave from Formia or Anzio. To reach Formio from Rome by car, take the Autostrada del Sole—A1 in the direction of Naples, exit at Frosinone, then take the provincial road for Terracina and continue for Formia. For Anzio take the provincial road Roma–Anzio. Anzio and Formia can both be reached by train from Rome. Aliscafo Vetor (T 07 71 700 710) operates hydrofoils from the harbours at Anzio and Formio about four times a day. The journey takes about seventy minutes.

Grand Hotel Santa Domitilla
Via Panoramica
04027 Isola di Ponza
T   07 71 80 9951/1
F   07 71 80 9955
E   info@santdomitilla.com
W   www.santadomitilla.com

Orestorante
Via Dietro la Chiesa 3
04027 Isola di Ponza
T   07 71 80 338
W   www.orestorante.it

FRASCATI [180]

By car, take the grande raccordo anulare junction for Naples; after 20 kilometres take exit 21–22 for Frascati and you will find yourself on the Via Tuscolana. From there Frascati is just 10 kilometres away. Trains leave Termini station every thirty minutes. Look for rail track number twenty-five. By subway, take Line A for Anagnina and then look for the bus to Frascati. alternatively a taxi ride will cost between €70 and 90.

Villa Grazioli
Via Umberto Pavoni 19
00046 Grottaferrata
T   06 94 54 001
F   06 94 13 506
E   info@villagrazioli.com
W   www.villagrazioli.com

Cacciani
Via Armando Diaz 13
00044 Frascati
T   06 94 20 378
F   06 94 20 440
W   www.cacciani.it

VILLA ADRIANA & VILLA D'ESTE [182]

If travelling by car, take the motorway A24 and then exit Tivoli; follow the road signs for Villa d'Este and Villa Adriana. By train, take the Rome to Pescara line and alight at Tivoli.

Villa Adriana
Via Villa Adriana 204
Tivoli
T   39 96 7900

Hotel Adriano
Via di Villa Adriana 194
00010 Villa Adriana Tivoli
T   07 74 53 5028
F   07 74 53 5122
W   www.hoteladriano.it

Villa d'Este
Piazzo Trento 1
00019 Tivoli
T   04 24 60 0460 for bookings
     from abroad
T   19 97 66 166 if telephoning
     within Italy
W   www.villadestetivoli.info
E   villadestetivoli@telekottage
     plus.com

SABAUDIA AND CIRCEO [184]

To reach Sabaudia by car from Rome, take the SS 148 towards Latina until you meet the crossway for Sabaudia. By train, take the Rome–Naples line and get off at Priverno Fossanova; from there a coach will take you to the centre of Sabaudia.

Complesso Punta Rossa
Via delle Batterie 37
04017 San Felice Circeo
T   07 73 54 8085/6/7/8
F   07 73 54 8075
E   punta_rossa@iol.it
W   www.puntarossa.it

Hotel Torre Paola
Via dei Casali di Paola
04016 Sabaudia
T   07 73 59 6947
F   07 73 59 6949
E   hotel@torrepaola.it
W   www.torrepaola.it

Saporetti
Via Lungomare
04016 Sabaudia
T   07 73 59 6024
E   ristorante@saporetti.com
W   www.saporetti.com